A Book of
Historical Recipes

A Book of Historical Recipes

Sara Paston-Williams

THE NATIONAL TRUST

Based upon *The Art of Dining: a History of Cooking and Eating*
first published in Great Britain in 1993 by National Trust Enterprises Limited,
36 Queen Anne's Gate, London S W1H 9A S

This edition first published in 1995.

British Library Cataloguing in Publication Data
A catalogue record for this book is available from the British Library.

ISBN 0 7078 0240 7

Original picture research by Samantha Wyndham; additional research by Gayle Mault
Designed by Newton Engert Partnership
Production management by Bob Towell

Phototypeset in Monotype Lasercomp Plantin 110
by Southern Positives and Negatives (SPAN), Lingfield, Surrey
Printed and bound in Hong Kong
Mandarin Offset Limited

Frontispiece: The dining-room at Kedleston, Derbyshire, designed by
Robert Adam in the 1760s. Bacchus, the tutelary deity of the 18th-century
dining-room, is carved on the marble chimney-piece, while the pictures
round the wall celebrate the pleasures of the table. On the sideboards
in the apse are wooden knife-boxes and a magnificent ormulu perfume
burner. A plate-warmer in the form of a Greek vase stands by the
fireplace, and two chestnut roasters, also in the form of Greek vases,
stand on the dining-table.

CONTENTS

Introduction

The 19th-century gastronome, Anthelme Brillat-Savarin, wrote 'Tell me what you eat and I will tell you what you are.' His words are borne out by this compilation of recipes, spanning the centuries from Richard II's court cooks, c.1400, to Brillat-Savarin's contemporaries, celebrated chefs such as Charles Elmé Francatelli and Auguste Escoffier. To redress the social balance are sources like the commonplace book of Elizabeth Birkett and the handwritten recipes of Mrs Straw.

The idea for the book came out of *The Art of Dining: a History of Cooking and Eating*, a project that dominated three years of my life and was published by the National Trust in November 1993. That book is large in every way: containing not only descriptions of how dishes were prepared, cooked and eaten, but also a great deal of food history to show what was available at different periods. We have now reduced this information right down – no cook would allow their sauce so to be treated – to provide a general introduction to five periods of history. We have taken the historical recipes included in *The Art of Dining*, amended some in the light of experience, and added extra recipes that could not be accommodated in the original book through lack of space. We hope that this book will inspire those who have not yet got a copy of *The Art of Dining*, to do so. Even those proud owners of a copy may find this mini-version more user-friendly in the kitchen!

All the kitchens, dining-rooms and other service rooms mentioned in this book are from National Trust properties, with the exception of Henry VIII's Privy Kitchen at Hampton Court, which is looked after by Historic Royal Palaces. Hampton Court is such an outstanding example of a Tudor kitchen that I couldn't leave it out, and as it can still be used on occasions for cooking, it forms the backdrop to the Elizabethan winter feast reproduced on the front cover.

I have drawn upon National Trust sources for original recipes whenever possible. This means that many of the recipes are reproduced for the first time, and cannot be found in other books. I have also tried to appeal to the modern palate, so roast peacock or swan do not feature! The ingredients in the adaptations of the historical recipes should be easily obtainable.

In *The Art of Dining* I acknowledged the help and support of many people at the National Trust together with archivists at local public record offices and food historians. I am obliged by pressure of space to repeat that blanket thank-you here.

Sara Paston-Williams, 1995

A detail from the painting of the life of Sir Henry Unton, c.1596. This shows Sir Henry and his guests at a banquet, the third course of dinner which, by late Elizabethan times, was often taken in a separate chamber. As they enjoy the sweetmeats and other delicacies laid before them, the diners are entertained by musicians and masquers.

Medieval and Early Tudor Food

For kitchens from this period to survive at all is remarkable. Inevitably they are mostly those of great households, like Bodiam Castle in Sussex (c.1400) or the Cistercian Fountains Abbey in Yorkshire (from 12th century onwards), both of which are roofless ruins. Later, more complete kitchens can be seen at Compton Castle in Devon (c.1520), Cotehele in Cornwall (refurbished 1520s) and Hampton Court Palace in Middlesex (King's Privy Kitchen, 1530s). Their distinctive features are loftiness, with high windows to prevent cross draughts, and one or more gigantic hearths for roasting and boiling, often with a baking oven attached.

Just as the hearth dominated kitchens, so meat dominated the diet of the wealthy and privileged. Favoured meats were beef, veal and mutton. Venison was highly prized, often given in pies as gifts. Rabbits were raised in warrens, pigeons in dovecotes – at Willington in Bedfordshire, for example, nesting boxes were provided for 1,500 birds.

Fish enjoyed almost as elevated a status, especially before the Reformation, when meat was forbidden on Fridays, Saturdays and Wednesdays, and during Lent. There was a wide range of fish to choose from, from porpoise to herrings, oysters to stockfish – although the last, dried cod, was a necessity rather than a pleasure. Sir William Petre's cook at Ingatestone Hall in Essex used a hammer to break up the pieces.

In the great roasting hearths, meat and fish were cooked on spits over the fire, and served with a sauce, usually vinegar-based, although ale, wine and milk were also used. I have given two sauce recipes: sauce madame, with wine as its base, for goose (p.11), and 'egerdouce' a sweet-sour sauce for fish (p.10).

On the boiling hearth would be set a cauldron, either hanging from hooks over the fire, or standing on its own stubby legs. In this was prepared pottage, an important component of medieval and early Tudor meals (recipe, p.10). The object was to produce a semi-liquid spoonmeat, either a 'running pottage' with chunks of meat or fish at the bottom of the bowl with broth above, or 'standing pottage' with a very thick consistency. For ordinary people, the pottage was based on the bread corn of the region; for the wealthy, there were rich spicy pottages of meat and fish called civey, gravey and blancmange.

Although a wide variety of vegetables and fruit was available during this period, they were suspected of being carriers of disease and inducers of melancholy. Fresh fruit like cherries and grapes were eaten at the beginning and end of meals to open and close the stomach, but vegetables and fruit were usually cooked long and hard.

Spices appear in every area of cookery. The traditional explanation for the generous use of spices in *haute cuisine* of this period is that they were essential to disguise the unpleasant taste of tainted or salted fish and meat. But it is clear from early manuscripts that spices were used just as much to flavour fresh meat and fish, and regular spicing was appreciated for itself as a status symbol. It is difficult to judge how heavy this spicing was – in contemporary manuscripts there are vague instructions to 'take cloves, ginger, cinnamon, pepper and sugar', but few recipes give any quantities. The result therefore was probably tasty rather than fiery.

Late medieval and early Tudor households, provided they had the wherewithal, ate three meals a day: breakfast at 6 or 7am, dinner at 11 or midday; supper between 5 and 6pm. Breakfast was a substantial meal, including bread, cold meats, fish, cheese, ale or wine, taken informally in one's chamber. Dinner was the most important meal of the day, consisting usually of two main courses made up of a number of dishes. First came the gross meats and fish, and pottages, followed by poultry, pies, puddings and salads. Supper tended to be a lighter form of dinner.

In the Middle Ages, formal dining took place in the great hall, or the refectory in religious houses. The high table, where the lord sat, was placed crossways, sometimes on a dais. Often a cloth of state was placed behind the lord's place to denote status. At Speke Hall, just outside Liverpool, and Rufford Old Hall in Lancashire, this has been translated into a great coved canopy. Other tables ran lengthways down the hall, usually on trestles that could be dismantled after meals. By the 16th century, however, the lord often ate in his great chamber with important guests, or his parlour with the family, while the steward presided in the great hall.

The following recipes are taken from three medieval cookery books. The *Forme of Cury* was compiled c.1390 by master cooks to Richard II, who was well known for his interest in food. The other two manuscripts are taken from the Harleian collection in the British Museum, while the last recipe, although dating from the 17th century, features a favourite medieval drink.

The coved canopy marking the high table at Rufford Old Hall.

Cawdel of muskels

'Take and seeth muskels [mussels]; pyke hem clene, and waisshe hem clene in wyne. Take almaundes & bray hem. Take somme of the muskels and grynde hem, & some hewe smale; drawe the muskels yground with the self broth. Wryng the almondes with faire water. Do alle thise togider; do therto verious [verjuice] and vyneger. Take whyte of lekes & perboile hem wel; wryng oute the water and hewe hem smale. Cast oile therto, with oynouns perboiled & mynced smale; do therto powdour fort, safroun & salt a lytel. Seeth it, not to stondying, & messe it forth.'

From the *Forme of Cury*, c.1390

Shellfish were a special treat during Lent: cooked either in a simple broth of their own juice with perhaps a little ale, or in rich spicy pottages like this recipe.

Spiced Mussel and Leek Broth

3 lb (1.5 kg) fresh mussels
2 tablespoons (30 ml) dry white wine
1 small onion, very finely chopped
8 oz (225 g) leeks, very finely sliced
2 tablespoons (30 ml) olive oil
1½ oz (40 g) ground almonds
2 teaspoons (10 ml) ground ginger
good pinch of saffron
¾ pt (450 ml) fish stock
salt and freshly milled black pepper
1 tablespoon (15 ml) white wine vinegar
4 tablespoons (60 ml) double cream

Thoroughly wash and scrub the mussels, scraping off any barnacles. Remove the beards and discard any mussels that do not close when given a good tap. Place in a large pan and add a dash of the wine. Cover with a lid and cook over a high heat for 4–5 minutes, shaking the pan until the mussels have opened. Strain the liquor through a colander into a bowl, reserving it. Heat the oil in a saucepan and soften the leeks and onions in it for about 3 minutes. Add the remaining wine and let it reduce by half. Stir in the ground almonds and spices. Mix the reserved cooking liquor with the fish stock and gradually add it to the pan, stirring well. Leave to simmer gently for 25 minutes.

Liquidise the soup and strain through a sieve into a clean saucepan. Taste and season as necessary, and sharpen with wine vinegar.

Discard one half of each mussel shell. Reheat the soup and stir in the cream and mussels. Serve immediately in bowls, with plenty of fresh crusty bread. Serves 4–6.

Egerdouce of Fysshe

'Take loches or roches other tenches other soles; smyte hem on pecys. Fry hem in oyle. Take half wyne, half vynegar, and sugur, & make a sirup; do therto oynouns icorue, raisouns coraunce, and grete raysouns. Do therto hole spices, gode powdours and salt; messe the fyssh & lay the sewe above and serve forth.'

From the *Forme of Cury*, c.1390

'Egerdouce' was a sweet-sour pottage in which kid, rabbit or sliced brawn was cooked, but it also provided a spicy sauce to accompany fried fish. The sour element came from the red wine or vinegar, the sweet from honey and dried fruits.

Sweet-Sour Sauce for Fish

6 fillets of sole
3 oz (75 g) butter
2 tablespoons (30 ml) olive oil

FOR THE SAUCE

2 tablespoons (30 ml) olive oil
3 oz (75 g) onions, chopped
1 oz (25 g) large raisins, stoned
1 oz (25 g) currants
½ teaspoon (2.5 ml) ground ginger
½ teaspoon (2.5 ml) ground mace
good pinch of ground cloves
½ teaspoon (2.5 ml) salt
1 oz (25 g) sugar
4 fl oz (120 ml) dry red wine
3 fl oz (90 ml) red wine vinegar
3 oz (75 g) fresh breadcrumbs
water

Make the sauce first. Gently cook the onions in the oil until soft, then add the dried fruit, spices and salt. Cook for a few minutes. Heat the sugar gently with the wine and wine vinegar in another saucepan until the sugar has dissolved, then add to the onion mixture. Simmer together, covered, for about 15 minutes, then liquidise in a blender or food processor. Return the sauce to a saucepan and stir in the breadcrumbs. Thin with a little water, then taste and adjust the seasoning as necessary.

Fry the fillets of sole in a little butter and oil and arrange on a hot serving plate. Serve the sauce separately. Serves 6.

Gees in sawse madame
'Take sawge [sage], persel [parsley], ysope [hyssop] and saueray [savoury], quinces and peeres [pears], garlek and grapes, and fylle the gees therwith; and sowe the hole that no grece come out, and roost hem wel, and kepe the grece that fallith thereof. Take galyntyne [meat juices thickened with breadcrumbs] and grece and do in a possynet [a three-legged cooking pot]. Whan the gees buth rosted ynowh, take hem of & smyte hem on pecys [cut into pieces], and take that that is withinne and do it in a possynet and put therinne wyne, if it be to thyk; do therto powdour of galyngale, powdour douce [a mixture of mild spices], and salt and boyle the sawse, and dresse the gees in disshes & lay the sewe onoward.'

From the *Forme of Cury*, c.1390

Roasted birds had their own sauces. The fresh fruit and herb stuffing of roast goose was mixed with wine and spices to make 'sauce madame' which was then poured over the bird. As a rule fresh fruit was regarded with great suspicion. Galingale can be bought in some specialist shops, otherwise use extra ginger. The sauce is also excellent with duck, venison, lamb, pork and chicken. Serve any left-over sauce with sausages – a delicious combination.

Roast Goose with Sauce Madame

10–12 lb (5–6 kg) oven-ready goose
salt and freshly milled pepper
sprig of fresh sage or ½ teaspoon (2.5 ml) dried
sprig of fresh hyssop or ½ teaspoon (2.5 ml) dried
sprig of fresh savoury or ½ teaspoon (2.5 ml) dried
2 teaspoons (10 ml) fresh parsley, chopped
4 tablespoons (60 ml) quince jelly
4 pears, peeled, cored and roughly chopped
4 oz (125 g) black grapes, seeded and halved
1 large garlic clove, crushed
7½ fl oz (225 ml) goose or chicken stock
7½ fl oz (225 ml) red wine
large pinch of ground ginger
½ teaspoon (2.5 ml) ground cinnamon
½ teaspoon (2.5 ml) grated nutmeg
large pinch of galingale (optional)

Preheat oven to 200°C, 400°F, gas mark 6. Sprinkle the body cavity of the goose with salt and black pepper and stuff with the herbs, quince jelly, fruit and garlic. Place on a rack in a roasting tin and prick all over with a cocktail stick. Rub with salt and pepper, then roast for 15 minutes per 1 lb (450 g) plus 15 minutes, or until the juices run clear.

When the goose is cooked, quickly carve it and keep the pieces hot on a serving dish in the oven while you make the sauce. (Alternatively, remove the whole goose to a warm serving dish and serve the sauce separately.)

Pour off any fat from the roasting tin, reserving the cooking juices. Spoon the stuffing from the carcase of the goose into the roasting tin, discarding the sprigs of fresh herbs. Add the stock and cook until reduced a little, then add the wine and the spices. Simmer for a few minutes, then taste and adjust the seasoning as necessary. Pour over the carved goose or into a jug and serve immediately. Serves 6–8.

Peiouns ystewed
'Take peiouns [pigeons] and stop hem with garlec ypylld [peeled] and with gode erbis ihewe [chopped herbs], and do hem in an erthen pot; cast therto gode broth and whyte grece [lard], powdour fort [a mixture of hot spices such as pepper and ginger], saffron, verious [verjuice] & salt.'

From the *Forme of Cury*, c.1390

Casseroled Pigeon with Herbs and Spices

4 oven-ready pigeons
12 large garlic cloves
4 teaspoons (20 ml) chopped fresh thyme
2 tablespoons (30 ml) chopped fresh parsley
salt and freshly milled black pepper
dripping or lard for frying
½ pt (300 ml) chicken stock
juice of ½ lemon
large pinch of ground ginger
pinch of saffron strands
½ teaspoon (2.5 ml) ground cinnamon
fresh herbs to garnish

Stuff each pigeon with 3 garlic cloves, 1 teaspoon (15 ml) chopped fresh thyme and ½ tablespoon (7½ ml) chopped fresh parsley. Season with a little salt and freshly milled black pepper, then brown the pigeons all over in a little dripping or lard in a heavy flame-proof casserole which is just big enough to take them. Pour over the stock, then add the lemon juice, ginger, saffron and cinnamon. Cover with a lid and cook in the centre of a moderate oven (180°C, 350°F, gas mark 4) for 1–1½ hours or until very tender. Taste the gravy and adjust the seasoning as necessary. Serve each person with a pigeon arranged on a slice of wholemeal toast with a little gravy poured over. Garnish with fresh herbs. Serves 4.

Crustade

'Take a cofyn, & bake hym drye; then take Marwbonys [marrow bones] & do ther-in; thenne nym hard yolkys of Eyroun [eggs], & grynde hem smal, & lye hem uppe with Milke; than nym raw yolkys of Eyroun, & melle hem a-mong chikonys y-smete [chopped chicken] & do ther-inne; & yf thou luste, Smal birdys; & a-force wyl thin comade with Sugre or hony; than take clowys [cloves], Mace, Pepir, & Safron, & put ther-to, & salt yt; & than bake, & serue forth.'

British Library *Harleian Ms 279, c.*1430

Wild and domestic birds provided variety and fresh meat in Britain's diet. For feasts, great pies were made of a number of the smaller birds mixed with marrow, egg yolks, dried fruit and spices.

Spiced Chicken and Pigeon Pie

FOR THE PASTRY

6 oz (175 g) wheatmeal flour
6 oz (175 g) white self-raising flour
pinch of salt
3 oz (75 g) margarine
3 oz (75 g) lard
cold water to mix

FOR THE FILLING

1 oven ready pigeon
¼ pt (150 ml) dry white wine
chicken stock
4 whole cloves
freshly milled black pepper
2 large chicken breasts
½ oz (15 g) butter
2 oz (50 g) button mushrooms, roughly chopped
1 oz (25 g) raisins
3 large eggs
salt and freshly milled black pepper
½ teaspoon (2.5 ml) ground ginger
½ teaspoon (2.5 ml) ground mace
pinch of powdered saffron
8 fl oz (240 ml) cooking liquor
beaten egg to glaze

First make the pastry. Sieve the flours and salt into a large mixing bowl. Lightly rub the fats into the flour until the mixture resembles fine crumbs. Sprinkle in enough cold water to form a smooth ball of dough that will leave the bowl clean. Knead lightly, then wrap in foil or polythene and chill in the fridge for 20 minutes. Roll out 8 oz (225 g) of the pastry and line a greased 8-in (20-cm) deep loose-bottomed flan tin or cake tin. Chill again for about 30 minutes.

Preheat oven to 200°C, 400°F, gas mark 6. Line the pastry case with foil or greaseproof paper and baking beans, place on a baking sheet and bake for about 25 minutes, removing the foil or paper and beans for the last five minutes. Remove the pastry case from the oven and leave to cool.

Meanwhile, to make the filling, place the pigeon in a flameproof casserole or saucepan. Pour over the wine and enough chicken stock to cover. Add the cloves and several grindings of black pepper, cover with a lid, then bring to the boil. Simmer very slowly for 1 hour, then add the chicken breasts and continue to cook for a further 45 minutes, or until the meat of both birds is really tender.

Remove the pigeon and chicken breasts from the stock and bone and skin them. Cut the flesh into small pieces. Cook the mushrooms gently in the butter, then mix with the meat, together with the raisins. Spread over the base of the pastry case. Beat the eggs thoroughly and season with salt, pepper, ginger, mace and saffron. Stir in the cooking liquor and pour over the meat.

Preheat oven to 180°C, 350°F, gas mark 4. Roll out the remaining pastry to make a lid. Dampen the edges, then fit it over the top of the pie. Seal the edges and make a steam-hole in the centre. Decorate with any remnants of pastry and brush with beaten egg. Place on a baking sheet and bake for about 35 minutes. Remove from the oven and serve warm. Serves 6.

The dovecote at Ightham Mote, Kent.

Chicken in Sauce of Three Colours

Capoun in Salome

'Take a Capon & skalde hym, Roste hym, then take thikke Almeunde mylke [almond-milk] temper it wyth wyne Whyte other Red; take a lytel Saunderys & a lytyl safroun, & make it a marbyl cloure, & so atte the dressoure throw on hym in ye kychoun, & throw the Mylke a-boue, & that is most commelyche, & serve fresh.'

British Library *Harleian Ms 279*, c.1430

Multi-coloured dishes like this were made for special occasions. A final garnishing with spice powder would take place at the dresser, before the dish was served at the second course.

3½–4 lb (1.75–2 kg) chicken
2 oz (50 g) ground almonds
1 oz (25 g) cornflour
¼ pt (50 ml) water
½ pt (300 ml) dry white wine
pinch of salt
red food colouring
little powdered saffron
little powdered cinnamon
little white pepper
little powdered mace
2 oz (50 g) whole almonds, blanched and fried gently in butter
few whole cloves

Roast the chicken in the normal way.

Blend the ground almonds with the cornflour and water, then stir in the wine. Pour into a saucepan and cook gently until the sauce comes to the boil, stirring continuously. Simmer for 10 minutes taking care it does not stick, then add salt to taste. Divide the sauce into three. Leave one-third white; colour one-third red with food colouring; colour the final third yellow with saffron. Keep the sauces warm until the chicken is cooked.

Skin and carve the cooked chicken into 8 pieces. Arrange on a hot serving dish and sprinkle with white pepper and powdered mace. Pour the three sauces into a large warm bowl and swirl together gently to make a marbled effect. Pour over the chicken and decorate with the fried almonds and a few whole cloves and serve immediately. Serves 4.

Herb and Flower Salad

Salat

'Take persel [parsley], sawge, grene garlec, chibolles [spring onions], oynouns, leek, borage, myntes, porrettes [a type of leek], fennel, and town cressis, rew, rosemaye, purslayne; lave and wasche hem clene. Pike hem. Pluk hem small with thyme hande, and mingle hem wel with rawe oile; lay on vynegar and salt, and serve it forth.'

From the *Forme of Cury*, c.1390

This is the earliest salad recipe in English. Mixed herb and flower salads proved so popular that they continued in fashion through to the 17th century. The salad would change according to the season and what grew in each cook's herb garden, so adapt and experiment with the basic recipe as you wish, as long as the result is colourful.

2 bunches watercress
1 carton mustard and cress
2 oz (50 g) fresh parsley in sprigs
1 small leek, finely sliced
6 spring onions, chopped
1 oz (25 g) sorrel leaves, coarsely chopped
1 oz (25 g) dandelion leaves, finely chopped
1 small bulb fennel, sliced into matchsticks
1 oz (25 g) daisy leaves, finely chopped
few red sage leaves
few mint leaves
1 sprig of fresh rosemary, chopped
1 garlic clove
1 tablespoon (15 ml) wine vinegar
sea salt and freshly milled black pepper
6 tablespoons (90 ml) olive oil
violets, primroses, daisies, blue borage flowers, dandelions and alexander buds to decorate.

Wash and dry all the salad stuff and prepare it. Mix together in a large bowl, which has been rubbed well with a garlic clove, reserving the flowers. Place the wine vinegar, seasoning and olive oil into a screw-topped jar and shake well to blend. Pour over the salad just before serving and mix again carefully. Decorate with flowers as you wish and serve immediately. Serves 6.

Tart in ymbre day

'Take and perboile oynouns & erbis & presse out the water & hewe hem smale. Take grene cheese & bray it in a morter, and temper it up with ayren [eggs]. Do therto butter, safroun & salt, and raisouns corauns, & a litel sugur with powdour douce [a mixture of mild spices], & bake it in a trap & serve it forth.'

From the *Forme of Cury*, c.1390

Ember days were among the Church's many days for fasting and prayer. The eating of meat was forbidden, but fish and 'white meats' (dairy products and eggs) were allowed. 'Green' cheese was new curd cheese which had to be eaten quickly because it was too damp to mature properly.

Char de coynes (charedequynce) or Chardwardon

'Take a quarter of clarefied hony, 3 ounces of pouder peper, and putte both togidre; then take 30 coynes [quinces], and 10 wardones [a type of large, hard pear], and pare hem, and drawe oute the corkes [cores] at eyther ende, and seth hem in goode wort til they be soft. Then bray hem in a morter; if they ben thik, putte a litull wyne to hem, and drawe hem thorgh a streynour; And then put the hony and that togidre, then sette al on the fire, and lete seth awhile til hit wex thikke, but sterre it well with 2 sturrers for sitting to; And then take it downe, and put there-to a quarter of an ounce of pouder ginger, And so moche of galingale, And so moche of pouder Canell [cinnamon], And lete it cole; then put hit in a box, And strawe pouder ginger and canell there-on.'

From the *Forme of Cury*, c.1390

Marmalade, from the Portuguese *marmelo* for quince, was a popular medieval confection in southern Europe. It was copied in England, at first under the Anglo-Norman name of 'chardecoynes' or 'chardequynce'. Quinces, or a mixture of quinces and warden pears, were boiled to a pulp, then cooked with wine, honey and plenty of spices to make a stiff paste which was then boxed for long keeping, to be eaten as a sweetmeat.

Quince marmalade remained a luxury gift until well into the 17th century.

Spiced Onion Tart

FOR THE PASTRY

3 oz (75 g) wholemeal flour
3 oz (75 g) white self-raising flour
pinch of salt
3 oz (75 g) butter
cold water

FOR THE FILLING

3 oz (75 g) butter
1 lb (450 g) large, mild onions, thinly sliced
2 tablespoons (30 ml) fresh parsley, finely chopped
1½ teaspoons (8 ml) fresh sage, finely chopped or ½ teaspoon (2.5 ml) dried
6 oz (175 g) curd cheese
2 medium eggs, lightly beaten
good pinch of ground cinnamon
good pinch of ground cloves
½ teaspoon (2.5 ml) ground ginger
½ teaspoon (2.5 ml) ground mace
salt and freshly milled black pepper
1½ oz (40 g) raisins

To make the pastry, sieve the flours and salt into a bowl, returning the bran left in the sieve to the bowl. Rub in the butter and sprinkle over enough water to make a smooth dough. Knead gently, then rest the pastry in the fridge for about 30 minutes.

Meanwhile, melt the butter in a large pan, add the onions and cook very gently until they are very soft and transparent, without browning. Remove the pan from the heat and stir in the parsley and sage.

Preheat oven to 190°C, 375°F, gas mark 5. Roll out the prepared pastry to line an 8-in (20-cm) flan tin, preferably loose-bottomed. Prick the base, line with greaseproof paper or foil and fill with baking beans. Bake on a preheated baking sheet for 15 minutes. Remove the beans and paper or foil and return the pastry case to the oven for 5 minutes to dry out. Remove from the oven and cool.

Preheat oven to 180°C, 350°F, gas mark 4. Mix the curd cheese with the lightly beaten eggs and spices, then add to the onion mixture. Season to taste. Put the pastry case on the hot baking sheet again and sprinkle in the raisins. Add the filling and bake for about 20 minutes, or until the filling is firm and lightly browned. Don't overcook or the tart may be dry. Serve warm or cold. Serves 6.

Quince Comfits

1 lb (450 g) very ripe quinces, cooking or crab apples, or pears, or a mixture of these fruits
¼ pt (150 ml) medium sweet white wine or water
about 1 lb (450 g) granulated sugar
little ground cinnamon, ground ginger, galingale (see p.11) and black pepper
caster sugar, to finish

Wash the fruit. If using quinces, rub off any of the grey fluff which may still be clinging to their yellow skins. Cut up roughly, including the skin and cores, and place in a heavy-based saucepan with the wine or water. Cover and simmer until very tender, then rub through a fine sieve. Weigh the pulp and return to a clean pan with an equal amount of granulated sugar. Season to taste with the spices, then bring slowly to the boil, stirring frequently to dissolve the sugar. Cook gently for about 1½ hours, or until very thick indeed and leaving the side of the pan. Stir fairly frequently to prevent the mixture sticking and burning on the bottom of the pan.

Remove from the heat and leave the mixture to cool completely, then roll small pieces in caster sugar. Store in an airtight container with extra caster sugar to prevent the sweets sticking together. Serve as sweetmeats with coffee after dinner. Makes about 30.

Crustard Lumbard in paste

'Take good creme, and yolkes And white of egges, and breke hem thereto, and streyne hem all thorgh a straynour till hit be so thik that it will bere him self; And take faire Mary [marrow], And Dates, cutte in 2 or 3 and prunes, and put hem in faire coffyns of paast [pastry cases]; And then put the coffyn in an oven, And lete hem bake till they be hard, And then drove hem oute, and putte the licoure into the Coffyns, And put hem into the oven ayen, And lete hem bake till they be ynogh, byt cast sugur and salt in the licour whan ye putte hit into the coffyns; And if hit be in lenton [Lent], take creme of Almondes, And leve the egges And the Mary.'

British Museum *Harleian Ms 4016, c.1450*

Flaunes and crustards were the ancestors of our modern flans and custards; delicious titbits of meat, vegetables, fish and fruit set with egg yolks and cream and baked in pastry cases (coffyns). Crustard Lumbard was considered fine enough to appear in the third course at Henry IV's coronation feast in 1399, with its filling of strained eggs and cream, sliced dates, prunes and marrow. In Lent, when rich dairy products were forbidden, almond milk or cream was used instead.

Rich Custard Pie with Date and Prunes

FOR THE PASTRY

8 oz (225 g) plain flour
5 oz (150 g) unsalted butter
½ oz (15 g) icing sugar
1 egg yolk
about 3 tablespoons (45 ml) cold water

FOR THE FILLING

1 level teaspoon (5 ml) cornflour
about 1 oz (25 g) caster sugar
3 large egg yolks
1 pt (600 ml) double cream
a good pinch of saffron
2 oz (50 g) stoned dates, chopped
2 oz (50 g) no-soak prunes, chopped

First make the pastry. Rub the butter into the flour and sieve in the sugar. Stir together, then beat the egg yolk with most of the cold water. Add to the mixture and work quickly to a firm dough with a fork, adding the remaining water if necessary. Do not overwork the pastry, but knead lightly until smooth.

Roll out on a lightly floured board and line a greased deep 8-in (20-cm) flan ring or cake tin with a loose bottom. Pinch the top edge to decorate, prick the base and leave to rest in a cool place for about 30 minutes.

Line the pastry case with foil or greaseproof paper and baking beans, place on a pre-heated baking sheet and bake in a fairly hot oven (200°C, 400°F, gas mark 6) for 25 minutes, removing the foil or paper and beans for the last 5 minutes.

Meanwhile, make the filling. Mix together the cornflour and the sugar in a bowl; add the egg yolks one at a time, beating until all the sugar has dissolved. Heat the cream with the saffron slowly until just on the point of boiling, stirring to get the best possible colour from the saffron. Allow to cool for about 5 minutes, then strain on to the egg mixture and whisk. Taste the custard and add more sugar if you like. Sprinkle the chopped dried fruit on to the pastry base and pour over the custard. Return to a moderate oven (180°C, 350°F, gas mark 4) for about 30 minutes or until just firm, but a little wobbly in the centre. Remove from the oven and cool. Serve slightly warm, or cold. Serves 6–8.

Sir Geoffrey Luttrell and his family at dinner, from the early 14th-century *Luttrell Psalter*.

Frutours

'Take yolkes of egges drawe hem together through a streynour, caste there-to faire floure, berme [brewer's yeast] and ale; stere it togidre til hit be thik. Take pared appelles, cut hem thyn like obleies [communion wafers], ley hem in the batur; then put hem into a ffrying pan, and fry hem in faire grece or butter til they be browne yelowe; then put hem in disshes, and strawe Sugur on hem ynogh, And serve them forthe.'

British Museum *Harleian Ms 4016, c.1450*

Egg-batter fritters raised with ale-barm regularly appeared in medieval menus, usually as part of the last course. Apple fritters, strewn with sugar when available, were perhaps the best loved, but fritters of root vegetables – skirrets, parsnips or 'pasternakes' – were well liked too.

Wardonys in Syrup

'Take wardonys [wardens or hard pears], and caste on a potte, and boyle hem till they ben tender; then take hem up and pare hem, and kyttle [cut] hem in two pecys; take y-now of powder of canel [cinnamon], a good quantyte, and caste it on red wyne, and draw it throw [through] a strynour; caste sugre ther-to, and put it [in] an erthen pot, and let it boyle: and thanne caste the perys [pears] ther-to, and let boyle togederys [together], and when they have boyle a whyle, take pouder of gyngere and caste ther-to, and a lytil venegre [vinegar], and a lytil safron; and loke that it be poynaunt and dowcet.'

British Museum *Harleian MS 279, c.1430*

Warden pears were hard and much larger than any other varieties.

Pears in Wine Syrup

6 large firm pears
about ¾ pt (450 ml) dry red wine
4 oz (125 g) caster sugar
½ teaspoon (2.5 ml) ground cinnamon
pinch of ground ginger
red food colouring (optional)
small bay leaves to decorate

Put the wine, sugar and spices in an enamel-lined or stainless steel saucepan just large enough to hold pears standing upright. Heat gently until the sugar has dissolved, then bring to the boil and simmer for 5 minutes.

Meanwhile, peel the pears as thinly as possible, leaving the stalks on. Core them from the base if you wish. Put the pears into the hot syrup, cover and simmer very gently for 20–30 minutes, or until just tender, basting them occasionally with the syrup. Transfer the pears to a serving dish with a slotted spoon. Taste the syrup and stir in a little more sugar to taste, then boil rapidly without covering until reduced by half and of a coating consistency. Cool a little, then spoon over the pears to give them an attractive reddish gleam. If the colour of the syrup does not seem bright enough, intensify it with 2 or 3 drops of red food colouring. Continue to baste the pears with the syrup until cold, then chill until ready to serve. Decorate with bay leaves stuck into the stalk ends of the pears. Serves 6.

Apple Fritters in Ale Batter

4 medium cooking or crisp, tart, eating apples
1 tablespoon (15 ml) lemon juice
caster sugar

FOR THE BATTER

4 oz (125 g) plain flour
½ teaspoon (2.5 ml) ground cinnamon
2 tablespoons (30 ml) sunflower oil
¼ pt (150 ml) pale ale, or still dry cider
2 egg whites
oil for deep-frying
caster sugar and ground cinnamon for
  sprinkling

Make the fritter batter first so that it has time to rest for at least 30 minutes before using. Sieve the flour and cinnamon together into a bowl. Make a well in the centre, pour the oil into this, followed by the pale ale or cider. Gradually beat the liquids into the dry ingredients, to make a smooth creamy batter. Set aside for 30 minutes.

When ready to cook, heat the oil for deep-frying to 190°C (375°F). Peel, core and slice the apples into ¼-in (7-mm) thick rings and sprinkle with lemon juice and caster sugar. Whisk the egg whites until stiff and fold them into the batter to make it extra light. Make the fritters in small batches, 3 or 4 at a time. Pat the apple slices with kitchen paper to mop up any excess lemon juice, dip them into the batter using a skewer or kitchen tongs, then shake off any excess batter. Lower carefully into the hot fat and fry for about 4 minutes or until golden brown and crisp. Drain well on kitchen paper and keep hot in a single, uncovered layer in the oven until all are cooked. Serve piping hot, dusted with caster sugar and cinnamon. Serves 6.

Gyngerbrede

'Take a quart of hony, & sethe it, & skeme it clene; take Safroun, poudir Pepir & throw ther-on; take gratyd Brede & make it so chargeaunt [thick] that it wol be y-leched; then take pouder Canelle [cinnamon] & straw ther-on y-now; then make yt square, lyke as thou wolt leche yt; take when thou lechyst hyt, an caste Box [garden box] leves a-bouyn, y-stykyd ther-on, on clowys [cloves]. And if thou wolt have it Red, coloure it with Saunderys [sandalwood] y-now.'

British Museum *Harleian Ms 279*, c.1430

Gingerbread, both red and white, was a favourite medieval sweetmeat. Home-made gingerbread could be prepared by mixing breadcrumbs to a stiff paste with honey, pepper, saffron and cinnamon. Ginger is omitted from the earliest recipe we have (see above), but this may be due to an accidental slip on the part of the scribe. Once made, it was shaped into a square, sliced and decorated with box leaves impaled on cloves.

Red and White Gingerbread

1 lb (450g) clear honey
tiny pinch of powdered saffron
1 teaspoon (5ml) ground black pepper
2 teaspoons (10ml) ground ginger
2 teaspoons (10ml) ground cinnamon
about 1 lb (450g) fresh white breadcrumbs
box leaves, or small bay leaves, and whole
 cloves to decorate

Warm the honey over a gentle heat until quite runny, then stir in the saffron and pepper. Pour into a large bowl and add the ginger and cinnamon, then mix in the breadcrumbs. It is impossible to say exactly how many bread-crumbs the honey will absorb because it varies, but the mixture should be very stiff. If not, add a few more breadcrumbs. Line a shallow gingerbread tin with baking parch-ment and press the mixture into it with your fingers. Level the top and leave to firm up in the fridge for several hours, then turn out on to another sheet of paper and cut into small squares. Arrange the gingerbread on a large plate, then decorate each square with two box or small bay leaves and a whole clove stuck in the centre. You can achieve an even prettier effect by gilding a few of the leaves or painting the ends of some of the cloves red.

If you want to achieve a chequerboard effect, make the mixture up in two lots, adding a few drops of red colouring to one quantity of honey before mixing, then con-tinue as before. Arrange the red and white squares of gingerbread alternately on the serving plate. Makes 12 servings.

To Make Ipocras

'Take a galon of claret or white wine and put there in 4 ounces of ginger, an ounce and half of nutmegs, of cloves, an quarter of Sugar, 4 pound. Let all this stand togeather in a pot at least twelve houers, then take it and put it in a clere bage made for the purpose so that the wine may come with good coller from the wine.'

From a manuscript at Erddig, c.1686

Hippocras, a rich sweetened and spiced wine drunk after meals, was still in vogue during the 17th century.

Spiced Red Wine

3 pt (1.5 litre) bottle dry red wine
8 oz (225g) granulated sugar
1 oz (25g) ground ginger
¼ oz (6g) ground cinnamon
¼ oz (6g) ground cloves

Heat the wine gently with the sugar until it has dissolved, stirring frequently. Mix in the spices, then allow to stand for 24 hours, stirring occasionally, then strain through a jelly bag or a double layer of muslin into a jug or bowl.

Pour back into the wine bottle and recork until needed. Makes 10–12 glasses.

A monk in the wine cellar,
from a 14th-century manuscript.

Elizabethan Food

As the 16th century progressed, so new gastronomic delights were added to the English table. Guinea fowl were imported from West Africa, while the turkey was named after the Turkey merchants who brought it from Central America. The first reference to turkey comes in a feast given by Archbishop Cranmer in 1541; thereafter it took off as a fashionable dish.

New fruit included the apricot from southern Europe, the melon from France, and the tomato from Mexico. Known as the love apple, the tomato was regarded as an aphrodisiac and was rarely used in cooking until the 18th century. Expeditions to the Americas yielded several new vegetables, including the kidney bean, native to Peru, most often served boiled and buttered as part of a salad. Previously the only beans known to Europeans were broad and soya: now Lima, scarlet runners, string and haricot as well as kidney beans became common. In 1564 John Hawkins brought back the sweet potato from Central America, and some twenty years later came the Virginia potato, confusingly from South America.

Elizabethan kitchens, like their medieval predecessors, were lofty, with high windows and stone-flagged floors, and are dominated by their hearths. Good National Trust examples from the mid-century are to be found at Buckland Abbey in Devon and Canons Ashby in Northamptonshire. But the state-of-the-art Elizabethan kitchen has to be Hardwick Hall in Derbyshire. When Bess of Hardwick built it in the 1590s, she had survived four husbands and overseen the construction of several houses.

The first cookery book to be printed in England, *A Proper Newe Booke of Cokerye*, was published c.1575 by an unknown hand. Thereafter cookery books proliferated – printed, as their titles suggest, to satisfy the demands for recipes from the wives of newly rich merchants: *The Good Huswife's Jewel* by Thomas Dawson, 1596; *The English Hus-wife*, by Gervase Markham, 1615; *A Delightful Daily Exercise for Ladies and Gentlewomen*, by John Murrell, 1621. Although some of the books were written in Stuart times, the dishes they describe are typically Elizabethan.

Several of the recipes I have reproduced are for the banquet or dessert course. Presentation of dishes for this special course was crucial. Gervase Markham in *The English Hus-wife* explains: 'you shall first send forth a dish made for show only [in sugar] a Beast, Bird, Fish, Fowl; then your Marchpane [marzipan], then preserved fruit, then a paste, then a wet sucket [crystallised fruit in syrup], then a dry sucket [candied fruits], Marmalade, comfets, apples, pears, wardens, oranges and lemons sliced . . .'. Many of these dishes were prepared in the still-room. There are no surviving examples of Elizabethan still-rooms, but an inventory taken at Dyrham Park, near Bath, in 1700 gives a clear picture of how such a room was organised: a pewter alembic to distil cordials and make rose-water; a small fire for sweetmeats and preserves; a stove or iron cupboard near the fire with shallow metal-lined shelves for stacking confections like wet and dry suckets, fruit marmalades and comfits.

The Elizabethans set great store by the visual impact of their food. Vivid colours were highly prized: green from the juice of spinach or parsley; yellow from saffron, egg yolks and marigold; red from sanders, a type of sandalwood from India, alkanet root and mulberrries; deep purple from indigo, turnsole and heliotrope; white from ground almonds and chicken; black from pounded figs and dates. For the very grandest effects, gold and silver leaf could be laid on the surfaces of gingerbreads and pies. For colourful effects in salads, fresh flowers were added (p.13), and flowers like borage, primroses and marigolds were combined in tarts (p.25).

The move from communal dining in the great hall gathered apace in Elizabethan times. The great hall continued its symbolic importance as the grand entrance to the house, as can be seen at Montacute in Somerset (1590s), Knole in Kent (remodelled from 1600), and above all at Hardwick Hall. On ordinary days, Bess would dine in her 'low great chamber' on the first floor, but for special guests, dinner would be served in the magnificent 'high great chamber' on the second floor, after the food was processed with great ceremony from the kitchen, through the hall and up the staircase that meanders across the house. For the banquet course, Bess would take her guests up to a special room on the roof of Hardwick so that they might enjoy the views of her demesne as well as the succulent sweetmeats and spiced wines that she had prepared for them.

The magnificent 'high great chamber' at Hardwick Hall, where Bess would entertain her most distinguished guests.

A Pudding in A Tench

'Take your Tench and drawe it very clene and cut it not over lowe. Then take beets boyled, or Spinage, and chop it with yolks of hard Eggs, Corance, grated Bread, Salt, Pepper, Sugar and Sinamon and yolks of rawe Egges, and mingle it togither, and put it in the Tenches belly. Then put it in a platter with faire water and sweet butter and turn it in the Platter and set it in the Oven, when it is inough: serve it with sippets and poure the licour that it was boiled in upon it.'

A Booke of Cookry Very Necessary for All such as Delight Therein, gathered by A. W., 1584

A Herring Pye

'Take white pickled Herrings of one nights watering and boyl a little. Then take off the skin, and take onely the backs of them, and pick the fish clean from the bones. Then take good store of Raisins of the Sun, and stone them, and put them to the fish. Then take a warden or two, and pare it, and slice it in small slices from the core, and put it likewise to the fish. Then with a very sharp shredding knife shred all as small and fine as may be: then put to it good store of Currants, Sugar, Cinamon, slic't Dates and so put it into the coffin with good store of very sweet Butter, and so cover it, and leave onely a round vent-hole on the Top of the lid, and so bake it like pies of that nature: When it is sufficiently bak't, draw it out, and take Claret Wine, and a little Verjuice, Sugar, Cinamon, and sweet Butter, and boyl them together: then put it in at the vent-hole, and shake the pye a little, and put it againe into the Oven for a little space, and so serve it up, the lid being candid over with Sugar, and the sides of the dish trimmed with Sugar.'

From *The English Hus-wife*, Gervase Markham, 1615

Whole Baked Salmon with a Spinach Stuffing

2–3 lb (1–1.5 kg) fresh salmon, carp or other
   freshwater fish, cleaned
salt and freshly milled black pepper
1 cup spinach, cooked and chopped
1 oz (25 g) fresh wholemeal breadcrumbs
large pinch of ground cinnamon
pinch of sugar
1 oz (25 g) currants
1 egg yolk
1½ tablespoons (22 ml) butter, melted
¼ pt (150 ml) dry white wine
2 slices of wholemeal bread, toasted and cut
   into triangles, to garnish
slices of orange and sprigs of fresh dill,
   to garnish

Preheat oven to 180°C, 350°F, gas mark 4. Sprinkle the cavity of the fish with salt and black pepper. In a bowl, mix together the spinach, breadcrumbs, cinnamon, sugar, currants and egg yolk. Season with salt and pepper. Use the mixture to stuff the fish and keep in place with wooden cocktail sticks or skewers. Place the fish in a buttered roasting tin and brush liberally with the melted butter. Pour the wine over the fish and bake uncovered for 30–40 minutes depending on the size, basting several times. Divide the fish into four portions, discarding all the skin, bones and head. Serve with the cooking juices poured over and garnished with toast, orange slices and dill. Serves 4.

Pickled Herring and Fruit Pie

FOR THE PASTRY

12 oz (350 g) plain flour
pinch of salt
freshly milled black pepper
3 oz (75 g) butter
3 oz (75 g) lard
cold water to mix

FOR THE FILLING

1 lb (450 g) pickled herrings or rollmops
1 large cooking pear, peeled, cored and sliced
1 oz (25 g) raisins
1 oz (25 g) currants
2 oz (50 g) dates, pitted and minced
pinch of salt
large pinch of ground cinnamon
2 tablespoons (30 ml) dry white wine
1 oz (25 g) butter, cut into small pieces
beaten egg, or milk, to glaze
1 teaspoon (5 ml) sugar

To make the pastry, sieve the flour and salt together into a bowl. Add a sprinkling of pepper, then rub in the butter and lard until the mixture resembles fine breadcrumbs. Mix with enough cold water to make a firm dough. Knead lightly until smooth, then chill for about 10 minutes.

Line a well-greased 8-in (20-cm) deep flan tin with half the chilled pastry and bake blind in a hot oven (210°C, 425°F, gas mark 7) for 10 minutes. Leave to cool.

Meanwhile, prepare the filling. Unroll the herrings if necessary and remove the onions if there are any, reserving them for later. Rinse the pickled herrings in cold water, then drain. Plunge them into 3 pt (1.5 litres) boiling water in a saucepan. Cook for 1 minute, then remove and drain well. Cut into chunks.

Mix the pear, raisins, currants, dates, salt, cinnamon and wine together in a bowl and add the herring. Drain off any excess liquid and transfer filling to pastry-lined flan tin. Dot the mixture with the butter, then roll out remaining pastry to make a lid. Decorate top with any pastry trimmings, then brush well with beaten egg or milk. Cut a vent in the lid to allow the steam to escape, then sprinkle it with sugar. Bake in a moderately hot oven (190°C, 375°F, gas mark 5) for 1 hour or until golden brown. Serves 4–6.

Beef Olive Pie

8 oz (225 g) shortcrust pastry
6 thin slices topside beef
14 oz (400 g) raw spinach and sorrel including
    a few violet and strawberry leaves if
    available, trimmed and washed
2 spring onions, finely chopped
1 teaspoon (5 ml) fresh thyme, chopped
2 fl oz (60 ml) red wine
½ teaspoon (2.5 ml) salt
2 hard-boiled eggs plus 1 hard-boiled egg yolk,
    finely chopped
extra 2 tablespoons (30 ml) red wine
1 oz (25 g) currants
large pinch of ground cinnamon
pinch of ground cloves
pinch of ground mace
2 oz (50 g) butter
1 oz (25 g) raisins
6 prunes, stoned and finely chopped

Preheat oven to 210°C, 425°F, gas mark 7. Roll out the pastry and use to line a 9-in (22.5-cm), deep flan dish. Bake for 10 minutes, then reduce the temperature to 180°C, 350°F, gas mark 4 and continue baking for another 5 minutes. Remove from the oven and set aside to cool.

Chop the prepared greenstuff and place with the spring onions, thyme and red wine in a large saucepan. Sprinkle with salt. Cover and cook over a high heat for about 3 minutes, or until the greens begin to wilt. Place in a colander to drain.

Beat out the meat until thin and flat. Set aside while preparing the stuffing. Place the chopped egg, wine, currants and spices in a bowl. Add 2 oz (50 g) of the wilted greens, chopped very fine and season with salt. Mix thoroughly. Divide the mixture equally into six and spread on each of the steaks. Top with a small piece of butter and roll up neatly. Secure with fine string or a cocktail stick.

Add the raisins and prunes to the remainder of the greenstuff and mix together well. Place the mixture in the prepared flan case. Arrange the stuffed 'olives' on the greens and dot with more butter. Cover tightly with kitchen foil and bake in a fairly hot oven (190°C, 375°F, gas mark 5) for 30–40 minutes, or until the beef is cooked.

Remove the foil and string or cocktail sticks and serve as though it were a pie. Serves 6.

Detail of marigolds and herbs from the herb garden in the South Orchard at Hardwick Hall.

Spicy Chicken in Orange Sauce

To boyle a Capon with Orenges after Mistress Duffelds Way

'Take a Capon and boyle it with Veale, or with a marie [marrow] bone, or what your fancy is. Then take a good quantitie of that brothe, and put it in an earthen pot by it selfe, and put thereto a good handfull of Currans, and as manie Prunes and a fewe whole maces, and some Marie, and put to this broth a good quantitie of white Wine or of Claret, and so let them seeth softlye together: Then take your Orenges, and with a Knife scrape of all the filthinesse of the outside of them. Then take them in the middest, and wring out the juyce of three or foure of them, put the juyce into your broth with the rest of your stuffe. Then slice your Orenges thinne, and have uppon the fire readie a skillet of faire seething water, and put your sliced Orenges into the water and when that water is bitter, have more readie, and so change them still as long as you can find the great bitternesse in the water, which will be five or seven times, or more. If you find need: then take them from the water, and let that runne cleane from them: then put close orenges into your potte with your broth, and so let them stew together till your Capon be readie. Then make your sops with this broth, and cast on a little Sinamon, Ginger and Sugar, and upon this lay Capon, and some of your Orenges upon it, and some of your Marie, and towarde the end of the boyling of your broth, put in a little Vergious, if you think best.'

From *The Good Huswives Handmaid for Cookerie in her Kitchin*, 1597

4–5 lb (1.8–2.25 kg) chicken, cut into 12 pieces
salt and freshly milled pepper
flour
1 oz (25 g) butter
1 tablespoon (15 ml) vegetable oil
¼ pt (150 ml) chicken stock
3 fl oz (90 ml) dry white wine
9 fl oz (270 ml) orange juice
2½ teaspoons (12.5 ml) dried orange peel
large pinch of ground mace
pinch of ground rosemary
pinch of ground cinnamon
pinch of ground ginger
1 teaspoon (5 ml) sugar
8 oz (225 g) prunes, stoned
2 oz (50 g) currants
6 slices wholemeal toast
orange slices to garnish

Dust the chicken pieces with seasoned flour. Heat the butter and oil in a heavy casserole and brown the chicken pieces all over, a few at a time, adding more fat as necessary. Remove them from the pan with a slotted spoon and set aside. Add all the other ingredients except toast and the orange slices to the casserole and mix together well. Replace the browned chicken pieces in the casserole, cover with a lid and place in a moderate oven (180°C, 350°F, gas mark 4) for 1–1½ hours, or until the chicken is tender. Adjust the seasoning as necessary and arrange the pieces of chicken on buttered toast. Spoon the orange sauce over and decorate with orange slices. Serves 6.

To Make Stewed Steakes

'Take a peece of Mutton, and cutte it in pieces, and wash it very cleane, and put it in a faire pot with ale, or with halfe Wine, then make it boyle, and skumme it cleyne, and put into your pot a faggot of Rosemary and Time, then some parsely picked fine, and some onyons cut round, and lit them all boyle together, and season it with sinamon and Ginger, Nutmeggs, two or three Cloves and salt, and so serve it on soppes and garnish it with fruite.'

From *The Good Huswifes Jewell*, Thomas Dawson, 1596

Oranges, a woodcut illustration from Gerard's *Herball*, 1597.

Lamb Casseroled in Ale with Prunes and Raisins

4 lamb leg steaks, approx. 1½ lb (675g)
1 oz (25g) butter
1 tablespoon (15 ml) vegetable oil
1 large onion, finely sliced
1 pint (600 ml) real ale
½ tablespoon (7.5 ml) fresh rosemary, chopped
*   or ½ teaspoon (2.5 ml) dried rosemary*
½ tablespoon (7.5 ml) fresh thyme, chopped
*   or ½ teaspoon (2.5 ml) dried thyme*
2 tablespoons (30 ml) fresh parsley, chopped
½ teaspoon (2.5 ml) ground allspice
2 or 3 whole cloves
2 oz (50g) raisins
freshly milled black pepper and salt
1 oz (25g) fresh white breadcrumbs
8 oz (225g) prunes, stoned
4 slices wholemeal toast
orange slices, to garnish

Heat the butter and oil in a heavy casserole dish and brown the lamb steaks quickly on both sides. Remove with a slotted spoon and set on one side. Reduce the heat and cook the onions in the remaining fat until soft. Replace the meat in the casserole and cover with ale. Add the herbs, spices and raisins, then season with salt and pepper. Cover tightly with a lid and place in a moderate oven (180°C, 350°F, gas mark 4) for 30 minutes. Add the bread-crumbs and prunes and return to the oven for a further 30 minutes, or until the lamb is tender. Check the seasoning and adjust as necessary, then serve each lamb steak on a slice of toast. Pour over the gravy and garnish with slices of orange, before serving. Serves 4.

To make Fritters of Spinnedge

'Take a good deale of Spinnedge, and wash it cleane. Then boile it in faire water, and when it is boiled, then take it forth and let the water runne from it. Then chop it with the backe of a knife, and then put in some egges and grated bread, and season it with sugar, sinamon, ginger and pepper, dates minced fine, and currants, and roule them like a ball, and dippe them in butter [batter] made of Ale and flower.'

From *The Good Huswifes Jewell*, Thomas Dawson, 1596

Fritters made from the pulped leaves of spinach, beets or clary, bugloss or lettuce were very popular. Spinach was also enjoyed as a boiled salad with currants.

Late 16th-century painted glass in the King's Room, Oxburgh Hall, Norfolk, showing the brewing of beer or ale.

Spinach and Date Fritters

1 lb (450g) fresh or frozen spinach
2 medium eggs
large pinch of salt
pinch of freshly milled pepper
large pinch of soft brown sugar
large pinch of ground cinnamon
large pinch of ground ginger
1 oz (25g) fresh white breadcrumbs
2 oz (50g) currants
2 oz (50g) finely minced dates

FOR THE BATTER

3 oz (75g) self-raising flour
pinch of salt
3 fl oz (90 ml) water
2 tablespoons (30 ml) light ale
vegetable oil for deep frying

Wash and trim the spinach if using fresh, and cook for 1–2 minutes, or until the leaves begin to wilt. If using frozen, cook gently until thawed. Drain in a colander and leave to cool, then chop finely. Squeeze out excess moisture. In a bowl, mix the eggs, seasoning, sugar, spices and breadcrumbs until well blended, then stir in the currants, dates and chopped spinach.

Prepare the batter by sieving the flour and salt into a bowl, then gradually whisk in the water and ale until smooth and free from lumps. The mixture should have the consistency of thick pancake batter. In a heavy frying pan, heat about ½-in (1.25-cm) of oil until it begins to smoke. Shape the spinach mixture into small patties, then place a few at a time in the prepared batter. Remove with a draining spoon, then fry for about 3 minutes on each side or until golden brown. Drain on kitchen paper, then serve hot as a snack with drinks or as a starter. Makes about 20 small fritters.

To Candy any Roots, Fruits or Flowers

'Dissolve sugar, or sugar-candy in Rose-water. Boile it to an height. Put in your roots, fruits or flowers, the sirrop being cold. Then rest a little, after take them out, and boyl the sirrop again. Then put in more roots, etc. Then boyl the sirrop the third time to an hardnesse, putting in more Sugar, but not Rose-water. Put in the roots, etc. the sirrop being cold, and let them stand till they candy.'

From *The English Hus-wife*, Gervase Markham, 1615

In contrast to the wet suckets, dry suckets or sucket candies were made by draining the fruit, roots, or flowers from their syrup and drying them.

Crystallised Fruit

1 lb (450g) suitable fruit, prepared
4 oz (125g) powdered glucose
2½ oz (60g) granulated sugar for initial boiling
about 14 oz (400g) granulated sugar for later boilings

Only perfect, firm, ripe fruit should be used and you get the best results by candying each type of fruit separately to keep the individual flavour. Some of the most successful are apricots, cherries, peaches, oranges, grapes and pineapple. Prepare them according to type: small, whole plums and apricots should be pricked all over with a stainless steel fork; cherries and grapes must be stoned; peaches and pears should be peeled and quartered; oranges and pineapple should be peeled and cut into suitable pieces. Chunks of parsnip and baby carrots are also successful.

Place the prepared fruit in a large saucepan and cover with boiling water. Simmer over a gentle heat until the fruit is just tender, but not broken up. This will vary with the type of fruit used. Remove the fruit carefully from the cooking liquor with a slotted spoon and place in a heatproof dish. Reserve the cooking liquor and measure out ½ pt (300ml) of this

into a saucepan with the glucose and 2½ oz (60g) sugar. Heat very gently, stirring all the time, until the sugar has dissolved. Then bring to the boil and pour the hot syrup over the fruit making sure that it is completely immersed. Cover and leave for 24 hours.

Place a sieve over a saucepan and carefully drain the syrup from the fruit into the saucepan. Return the fruit to the ovenproof dish. Add another 2 oz (50g) sugar to the syrup, stir over a gentle heat until this has dissolved, then bring to the boil. Pour over the fruit, cover and leave for a further 24 hours. Repeat the process three more times adding another 2 oz (50g) sugar each time.

Carefully drain the syrup from the fruit into a saucepan as before. Add 3 oz (75g) sugar to the syrup, place saucepan over a gentle heat and stir until the sugar has dissolved, then add the fruit and simmer for 3 minutes. Return the fruit and syrup to the heatproof dish. Cover and leave for 48 hours. Repeat the process. The syrup should now be as thick as clear honey. If the syrup is too thin at this stage, add another 3 oz (75g) sugar to the syrup, dissolve the sugar over a gentle heat, then add the fruit and simmer for 3 minutes. Leave the fruit to soak in the thick syrup for 4 days. Remove the fruit carefully from the syrup with a draining spoon and lay it on a wire rack, placed over a baking tray to catch the drips.

To dry off the fruit, place the tray in a warm place, turning the fruit occasionally during the drying process. The fruit is candied when the surface is no longer sticky. To finish it off, sprinkle some granulated sugar on grease-proof or waxed paper. Lift up each piece of candied fruit on a fine skewer and quickly dip it into boiling water. Allow to drain for a couple of seconds, then roll each piece in sugar until it is evenly, but not thickly coated. Leave to dry on a wire rack.

Serve piled in bowl-shaped champagne glasses, or sundae dishes, as a dessert with fresh cream, yoghurt or ice-cream.

Shred Pyes

'Take 4 pound of a legg of veal parboyled, 4 pound of Beefe suet, 6 pared Aples. Shred altogether, put it through a sieve, season it with 4 pound of Currans, an ounce of beaten Mace, halfe a pound of sugar, six dates, Lemon Pills candyed, a Gill of Rose Watter, as much sack; make them up; a quarter of an hour will bake them.'

From a commonplace book of recipes dated 1699, belonging to Elizabeth Birkett of Townend, Cumbria.

The recipe for these *shred* or *minced* pies harks back to Elizabethan times when they had already become part of traditional Christmas fare. Most mincemeat recipes until the 20th century included a little chopped meat, sometimes raw, sometimes cooked.

Mince Pies

8 oz (225g) cooked lean veal or beef
8 oz (225g) cooking apples
8 oz (225g) large raisins, stoned
2 oz (50g) dates, stoned
8 oz (225g) shredded beef suet
8 oz (225g) currants
1 oz (25g) candied lemon peel, finely chopped
2 level teaspoons (10ml) ground mace
1 tablespoon (15ml) sugar
3 tablespoons (45ml) rose-water
3 tablespoons (45ml) sherry

Mince the meat, cooking apples, raisins and dates into a bowl. Add the suet, currants, peel, spice and sugar and mix together well. Moisten with the rose-water and sherry. Put a spoonful of mincemeat in patty tins lined with shortcrust or puff pastry. Brush the edges of the pastry with beaten egg white and add pastry lids, pinching the two edges together. Make a small slit in the centre of each pie and glaze the top with egg white. Sprinkle with sugar and bake in a hot oven (220°C, 425°F, gas mark 7) for 15–20 minutes. Serve warm. Makes 2½–3 lb (1–1.4kg) mincemeat.

A Tarte of Borage Flowers

'Take borage floures and perboyle them tender, then strayne them wyth the yolkes of three or foure egges, and swete curdes, or els take three or foure apples and perboyle wythal and strayne them with swete butter and a lyttle mace and so bake it.'

To Make a Tarte of Marigoldes, Prymroses or Couslips

'Take the same stuffe to every of them that you do to the tarte of borage and the same ceasonynge.'

To Make Short Paest For Tarte

'Take fyne floure and a cursey [cup] of fayre water and a dyshe of swete butter and a lyttel saffron, and the yolkes of two egges and make it thynne and as tender as ye maye.'

From *A Proper Newe Booke of Cokerye*. This book, compiled by an unknown hand, probably before 1572, once belonged to the Tudor prelate, Archbishop Parker.

Tarts of flowers were prepared during spring and summer. Cowslips, primroses, borage flowers or marigold petals were beaten small and combined with eggs and cream or curds, then baked in a pastry case. They were served at the second course or the banquet.

Marigolds, a woodcut from Gerard's *Herball*.

Marigold Tart

FOR THE PASTRY

½ teaspoon (2.5 ml) saffron strands
1 tablespoon (15 ml) warm water
8 oz (225 g) plain flour
2 tablespoons (30 ml) icing sugar
5 oz (150 g) unsalted butter
2 egg yolks

FOR THE FILLING

3 tablespoons (45 ml) dried marigold petals
  (removed from the heads)
water
2 oz (50 g) caster sugar
8 oz (225 g) cream cheese or fromage frais
2 eggs, separated
3 tablespoons (45 ml) single cream
finely grated rind of 1 orange
1 oz (25 g) plain flour
crystallised borage flowers to decorate

Make the pastry first. Crumble the saffron in warm water in a basin and leave until cold.

Sieve the flour and icing sugar together into a bowl, then cut and rub in the butter until it forms fine crumbs. Beat the egg yolks with the saffron water and add to the rubbed-in mixture until it forms a firm dough. Knead lightly until smooth, then wrap in foil or plastic and chill in the fridge for at least 30 minutes. Then roll out the pastry and line a greased 9–10 in (23–25.5 cm) loose-bottomed flan tin. Prick the base lightly with a fork.

To make the filling, bring a small saucepan of water to simmering point and sprinkle in the marigold petals. Wet thoroughly, then drain and reserve. Beat the sugar with the cream cheese or fromage frais until soft and smooth, then beat in the egg yolks, one at a time, followed by the cream. Stir in the grated orange rind, the marigold petals and the flour. Whisk the egg whites until thick, then fold them into the cream cheese and egg yolk mixture. Pour into the pastry case and cook in the centre of a fairly hot oven (200°C, 400°F, gas mark 6) for 35–40 minutes, or until firm to the touch in the centre. If the top is getting too brown, lay some foil gently over it.

Leave the tart to cool a little in the tin, then loosen the sides with a knife, and transfer to a serving plate. Decorate with crystallised borage flowers and serve lukewarm. Serves 8.

To Make a Dyschefull of Snowe

'Take a pottell [half a gallon] of swete thycke creame and the whytes of eyghte egges, and beate them altogether wyth a spone. Then putte them in youre creame and a saucerful of Rosewater, and a dyshe full of Suger wyth all. Then take a stycke and make it cleane, and then cutte it in the ende foure square, and therwith beate all the aforesayde thynges together, and ever as it ryseth take it of and put it into a Collaunder. This done, take one apple and set it in the myddes of it, and a thicke bushe of Rosemary, and set it in the myddes of the platter. Then cast your Snowe upon the Rosemary and fyll your platter therwith. And yf you have wafers caste some in wyth all and thus serve them forthe.'

From *A Proper Newe Booke of Cokerye*, c.1572

The greatest innovation in Elizabethan cookery was the discovery of eggs as a raising agent. Whites of eggs produced 'Snowe', a centrepiece for the banquet.

Apple Snow

1½ lb (675 g) cooking apples, peeled, cored and
  sliced
1 tablespoon (15 ml) rose-water
caster sugar, to taste
3 egg whites
3 oz (75 g) caster sugar
¼ pt (150 ml) whipping cream
sprigs of fresh rosemary to decorate
gold dragees to decorate

Cook the sliced apples with the rose-water until soft, then rub them through a fine sieve to make a smooth purée. Taste and sweeten with a little sugar if necessary. Leave to get cold, then measure out about ½ pt (300 ml).

In a large clean bowl, beat the egg whites until they stand in soft peaks. Gradually beat in the caster sugar and continue to beat to a stiff, glossy meringue. Gently fold in the measured apple purée, then spoon into individual glasses or sundae dishes. Top with swirls of whipped cream and decorate with rosemary and gold dragees. Serves 4–6.

To make Jombils a hundred

'Take twenty Egges and put them into a pot both the yolkes and the white, beat them wel, then take a pound of beaten suger and put to them, and stirre them wel together, then put to it a quarter of a peck of flower, and make a hard paste thereof, and then with Anniseeds moulde it well, ane make it in little rowles beeing long, and tye them in knots, and wet the ends in Rosewater; then put them into a pan of seething water, but even in one waum, then take them out with a Skimmer and lay them in a cloth to drie, this being don lay them in a tart panne, the bottome beeing oyled, then put them into a temperat Oven for one howre, turning them often in the Oven.'

From *The Good Huswifes Jewell*, Thomas Dawson, 1596

To Make Muscadines, commonly called Kissing Comfits

'Then slicke a sheet of white paper, slicked with a slick-stone very smooth, and rowle your sugar paste upon it, then cut it like lozenges with rowel, so dry them upon a stone, and when they bee dry they will serve to garnish a marchpaine, or other dishes, tarts, custards, or whatsoever else, if you will have any red you must mingle Rosa Paris, if blew bottles growing in the corn [cornflowers].'

From *A Delightfull Daily Exercise for Ladies and Gentlewomen*, John Murrell, 1621

Sugar plate, a kind of uncooked fondant, was moulded into all manner of objects for banquets. It could be coloured with flower juices and spices.

To make sucade of peeles of Lemmons

'First take off your peeles by quarters and seeth them in faire water, from three quartes to three pintes, then take them out, and put to as much more water, and seeth them likewise, and doo againe, till the water wherein they are sodden have no bitterness at all of the peeles, then you are ready, now prepare a Sirop the same liquor . . . one pint of rosewater, and for every quart of liquor one half pound of sugar; seethe them againe together on a soft fire of coles till the Sugar bee incorporated with the liquor, then put in your peeles, let them seeth softly till you percieve that your sirop is as thicke as like hony. Put them in a pot of stone.'

From *The Treasurie of Commodious Conceits and Hidden Secrets*, John Partridge, 1584

Jumbles or Knot Biscuits

1½ oz (40 g) salted butter
4 oz (125 g) caster sugar
1 tablespoon (15 ml) rose-water
½ oz (15 g) caraway seeds
1 large egg, beaten
8 oz (225 g) plain flour
extra rose-water and caster sugar for glazing

Preheat oven to 180°C, 350°F, gas mark 4. Cream the butter, sugar and rose-water together, then mix in the caraway seeds, beaten egg and flour to form a soft dough. Knead on a lightly floured board, then take small walnut-sized pieces of dough and with your fingers form each into a roll, approximately ¼-in (5-mm) in diameter and 6-in (15-cm) in length. Make into simple knots, plaits or rings and arrange on lightly greased baking sheets. Brush with rose-water and sprinkle with caster sugar. Bake near the top of the oven for about 20 minutes, or until tinged with brown. (Knots and plaits will take longer to bake than simple rings, so don't mix shapes on a baking sheet.) Remove from the oven and cool on a wire rack. Store in an airtight tin. Delicious served with syllabub (see page 35). Makes about 30.

Kissing Comfits

1 heaped teaspoon (8 ml) gum tragacanth
2 tablespoons (30 ml) rose-water
1 lb (450 g) icing sugar
1 oz (25 g) cornflour
extra rose-water
food colouring

Steep the gum tragacanth in the rose-water overnight until it has dissolved to form a sticky paste.

The next day sieve the icing sugar with the cornflour into a bowl. Work the paste into the icing sugar with a wooden spoon, gradually adding more rose-water until you have a smooth pliable modelling dough.

Divide the dough into portions and colour with red, blue, yellow and green colouring, leaving one portion uncoloured. Roll out thinly on a smooth surface, lightly dusted with cornflour and cut out with small fancy cutters. Leave to dry in a warm place, then serve as sweets, or use to decorate a marchpane (see p.27), tarts (see p.25) and custards (see p.15). Makes 1 lb (450 g) sweets.

Lemon or Orange Sucket

3 large lemons or oranges
1 pt (600 ml) cold water
14 oz (400 g) granulated or preserving sugar
2 tablespoons (30 ml) rose-water

Halve the lemons or oranges and squeeze out the juice, reserving it for some other use. Cut into quarters and scrape out any remaining pulp. Place the rinds in a saucepan with the water and boil for 30 minutes, changing the water three times during this boiling time to remove any bitter taste. The rinds should be very tender.

Place the sugar, rose-water and ¾ pt (450 ml) of the water from the last boiling in another saucepan. Heat very gently until all the sugar is dissolved, then bring to the boil. After draining any remaining liquor from the rinds, add them to the syrup and simmer until they are translucent and the syrup is as thick as thin honey. Spoon into warm sterilised jars and cover as for jam. Store until required. Serve with ice-cream, yoghurt or whipped cream. Serves 6.

How to make Marchpane Cake

'Take blancht Almonds and sugar and beat them up into a Past, and when have beaten it into a Past, rowl it out about the thickness that you will have your Marchpane Cakes to be and cut them in 3 square pieces and set an Edge to them of the same past, and Impress the Edges of them, then take Rose Watter and beat searced sugar in it till it be as thick as Pancakes, butter and wet them within it and strew a few of Bisketts in them and set them upon Wafers, and set them againe upon Papers and bake them, and keep them for your use.'

From a commonplace book dated 1699, belonging to Elizabeth Birkett of Townend, Cumbria.

To gild a Marchpane or any other kind of Tart

'Take and cut your leafe of golde, as it lieth upon the booke, into square peeces like Dice and with a Conies tailes end moysted a little, take golde up by the one corner, lay it on the place beeing first made moyste, and with another tayle of a Conie drie presse the golde downe close. And if ye will have the forme of an Harte, or the name of Iesus, or any other thing whatsoever: cut the same through a peece of paper and lay the paper upon your Marchpane or Tart; then make the voide place of the Paper (through which the Marchpane appeareth) moyste with Rose Water, laye on your golde, presse it down, take off your Paper and there remaineth behinde in golde the print cut in the saide paper.'

From *The Treasurie of Commodious Conceits and Hidden Secrets*, John Partridge, 1584.

The marchpane was the centrepiece of any banquet. It was a large flat disc of marzipan, sometimes with a raised rim round the edge, weighing perhaps 3–4 lb (1.5–1.8 kg) or more, which was iced, sumptuously decorated and surmounted for special occasions with three-dimensional figures or models in cast sugar (hot sugar syrup moulded in stone, wooden or pewter shapes); sugar plate (similar to modern fondant icing) or almond paste. Finally, the marchpane was often gilded with gold leaf, readily available but exceedingly expensive in Elizabethan times.

Gilded Marchpane

FOR THE MARCHPANE

1 lb (450 g) ground almonds
8 oz (225 g) caster sugar
3 tablespoons (45 ml) rose-water

FOR THE GLAZE

1 tablespoon (15 ml) rose-water
3 tablespoons (45 ml) icing sugar

Preheat oven to 150°C, 300°F, gas mark 2. Work the ground almonds, sugar and rose-water together to make a stiff paste. Knead until quite smooth. Reserve a little of the marzipan for decorating the marchpane and place the rest on a sheet of greaseproof paper. Roll it into a circle, about $\frac{3}{8}$-in (8-mm) thick, and decorate the edges with the back of a knife as you would a pie. Slip the marzipan on to a baking sheet and bake for 15 minutes, then turn off the oven, open the oven door and leave to cook for another 15 minutes, or until firm and dry, but only lightly coloured.

Meanwhile, mix the rose-water and icing sugar to a thin paste for the glaze. Brush over the marchpane and continue cooking for about 5 minutes until dry and glossy. Remove from the oven and leave to cool.

Roll out the reserved marzipan until quite thin and cut out into hearts, diamonds, letters, animals or birds. Paint with edible gold colouring and fix on to the glazed marchpane as it dries to form patterns or pictures. Alternatively, the reserved marzipan can be modelled into figures of animals or birds, or into knots which can be gilded as before. Sugar-coated caraway, fennel or coriander seeds, or confectioners' silver balls can also be used for decoration. Serve as a sweetmeat with coffee at the end of a meal.

A marchpane cake decorated with gold hearts, and wafers.

Stuart Food

With the Stuart dynasty on the English throne, closer links were forged with Europe: the marriage of Charles I to the French princess Henrietta Maria in 1625; exile in France and Holland for many members of the Court following the collapse of the royalist cause in the Civil War; and the marriage of Charles II to the Portuguese princess Catherine of Braganza in 1662. Gastronomy was affected just as much as politics.

When Elizabeth Dysart married John Maitland, Duke of Lauderdale, in 1672, she began to refurbish Ham House in Richmond, Surrey. Lauderdale was one of Charles II's chief ministers, while Elizabeth was a leading figure at the Restoration Court, so the redecoration and rearrangement of Ham was carried out in the latest style. No longer was it fashionable to have a great hall running across the centre of the house with the kitchen behind a screens passage. Instead, the ground floor should be raised, approached by a flight of steps, leaving a lofty basement storey below for the domestic offices. The kitchen in the basement at Ham is a light, airy room even though the ceiling is lower than in earlier kitchens.

Activity still centred round the broad-arched fireplace, but in wealthy households with good transport, coal was replacing wood. As it is impossible to kindle coal on a flat hearth, a fire basket was used instead. At Ham there is an iron hob grate with a moveable side, so the cook could alter the fire's dimensions. Alongside the fireplace were stewing hearths. Once the fire baskets had been filled with glowing charcoal, they gave easily controlled heat, vital for the fashionable 'made' dishes which M. Blangy, the Lauderdales' French cook, would have prepared. These dishes included fricassées – for example, chopped cold mutton, fried in sweet butter with white wine, salt and ginger; hashes – sliced fresh meat stewed with herbs, spices, broth and wine; and quelquechoses, which the English translated as 'kickshaws'. Although the recipe on p.31 is called Scotch Collops, the dish is cooked after the French fashion.

Ham, however, was a very fashionable household. Compare it to Townend in Cumbria, a moderately prosperous farmer's house of the same period, for instance, and Ham can be seen as way ahead of its time. The Brownes of Townend would not have included many French dishes in their dinners, although I have included the Scotch Collops recipe from the commonplace book of Elizabeth Birkett, who married into the family. Misson, a Swiss traveller to England in the 1690s, observed: 'Generally speaking the English tables are not delicately served. There are some Noblemen who have both French and English cooks, and these eat after the French manner, but among the Middling Sort they have ten or twelve sorts of common meals which infallibly take their turn at this Table, and two Dishes are their Dinner, a Pudding for instance and a fine piece of roast beef.'

The great British institution, the suet pudding, was made possible with the development of the pudding cloth, first recorded in a recipe of 1617 for 'Cambridge Pudding'. In the bakehouse other kinds of puddings were prepared. Once the cook had baked his or her bread in the hot oven, they could begin the baking of rich pies, patties, pastries and 'pudding pies' (puddings baked in a pastry case). As the oven cooled further, a variety of puddings could be baked slowly in specially turned wooden dishes: rich rice puddings including spices, rose-water, egg yolks, marrow and ambergris; whitepots made with cream, eggs, breadcrumbs or rice, dried fruits and spices (p.34); and custards. Great cakes containing dried fruit or caraway comfits and raised with ale barm were also cooked in the cooling bread oven. By the end of the 17th century the tin hoop had come into use to hold the cake in shape and help it to rise evenly (p.36).

Seventeenth-century meal times were later than their Tudor counterparts: breakfast at 9.30 or 10am, dinner at 2pm and supper at 7pm. By the end of the century the 'Continental' style of breakfast was enjoyed by the fashionable, with rolls, spiced bread and cakes served with the three 'strong bitter brews' introduced into England in the 1650s – coffee, chocolate and tea.

Tea-drinking 'Chinese style' after dinner also became a fashionable pastime, introduced into England by Catherine of Braganza. The Duchess of Lauderdale entertained her close friends in a richly decorated closet attached to her bedchamber. As the tea was extremely expensive, it was kept locked in a miniature cabinet of Chinese incised lacquer, and the Duchess would blend the leaves to her own proportions, brewing it in a teapot to be served in elegant little 'dishes' of porcelain.

A typical Stuart supper might consist of roast mutton or poultry, cold bacon, game pie, fish, cheesecakes, sweetmeats and fruit, served with spiced wines such as sack posset (p.37). Samuel Pepys in his diary for 1663 records a supper of 'good sack-posset and cold meats', after which he sent his guests home 'by about 10 o'clock at night'.

The Duchess of Lauderdale's Closet, Ham House.

To roast a Pike

'Take your pike and rub him well with salt, then take forth his Gutts and cut out of his belly. Then take a good quantity of sweet herbs. If your Pike is large put in the greater quantity of all these things that are here named, a quantity of Garlicke, take some Anchovyse, and some butter and all sortes of spices beaten togeether, mix these and fill his belly full and for spike him on the spit, and that which spares of filling his belly, put it on a dish and a little wine, and baste him with it, then put all on the dish with him and send him up in that sauce, you may after put in a quantity of pickled Herrings.'

From a commonplace book of recipes, medicinal, domestic and culinary of 1699, belonging to Elizabeth Birkett from Townend in Cumbria.

Freshwater fish, including pike from nearby Lake Windermere, would have been abundant at Townend. Pike was roasted on a spit in front of the fire with a stuffing of butter, highly flavoured with herbs, garlic, spices, pickled oysters and anchovies in its belly, which was later served up as a sauce to accompany the fish at the first course of dinner.

To Rost Venison

'After you have washed your venison clear from the blood, stick it with cloves on the outside and lard it with mutton larde or porke larde, but mutton is the best. Then spit it and rost it by a socking [slow] fire. Take vinegar, bread crums and the gravy which comes from the venison and boyle them in a dishe, then season it with sugare, cinamon, ginger and salt, and serve the venison upon the sauce.'

Erddig MS 1203, c.1685

The venison eaten at Erddig came from the deer park at Chirk Castle. Venison was highly prized by the gentry in the 17th century and brought social cachet to anyone able to offer it to guests. The roast venison of Stuart England was well larded, if lean, and stuck with cloves or sprigs of rosemary. A sugared and spiced wine and vinegar sauce, thickened with breadcrumbs, was commonly served with it.

Roast Venison with Cloves

3½–4½ lb (1.65–2 kg) haunch venison
6 oz (175 g) butter, softened
few whole cloves
1 oz (25 g) plain flour
sprigs of fresh rosemary to decorate

FOR THE MARINADE

½ pt (300 ml) red wine
1 carrot, peeled and sliced
1 medium onion, sliced
1 sprig of fresh thyme
1 bay leaf
pinch of ground cinnamon
pinch of ground ginger
1 teaspoon (5 ml) black peppercorns
2 tablespoons (30 ml) red wine vinegar
2 tablespoons (30 ml) olive oil
1 clove garlic
2 teaspoons (10 ml) soft brown sugar

The day before you intend to serve the venison, place all the marinade ingredients in a saucepan and bring to the boil. Boil for 20 minutes, then allow to cool.

Place the venison in a large china bowl, pour over the marinade and stand in a cool place for 24 hours. Turn the joint and spoon the marinade over it from time to time.

When ready to cook the venison, remove it from the marinade. Spread it with the softened butter, stick it with a few cloves and lay it in a roasting tin. Roast in a moderate oven (180°C, 350°F, gas mark 4) for 2–2½ hours, basting several times during cooking.

Remove the venison from the roasting tin and keep warm on a serving dish. Pour off any surplus fat from the tin and stir the flour into the pan juices over a gentle heat. Strain the marinade liquor and add it very gradually to the roasting tin stirring continuously until smooth. Taste for seasoning and adjust as necessary, then simmer for 5 minutes. Serve the sauce separately. Decorate the venison with sprigs of rosemary. Serves 6.

Pike in Red Wine with Anchovy

2–3 lb (1–1.5 kg) pike, cleaned but not scaled (Note: cod may be used instead)
salt and freshly milled black pepper
1 sprig each parsley, thyme, marjoram and rosemary
blade of mace
1 garlic clove
a little flour
2 oz (50 g) anchovies
8 oz (225 g) melted butter
½ pt (300 ml) claret
fresh herbs to garnish

Sprinkle the inside of the fish with salt and pepper and add the fresh herbs, mace and garlic. Rub the fish all over with flour, salt and pepper and lay it in a buttered ovenproof dish. Place the anchovies with the melted butter and claret in a saucepan, heating gently to dissolve them. Pour over the fish and bake in a fairly hot oven (190°C, 375°F, gas mark 5) for about 35 minutes, basting from time to time. Test with a skewer; the flesh should move easily from the backbone.

Lift the fish very carefully on to a warm serving plate, remove the stuffing and discard. Strain the sauce, taste and adjust seasoning as necessary, then pour over the waiting fish. Garnish with fresh herbs. Serves 6.

A detail of fish from the carving attributed to Grinling Gibbons in the King's Room, Oxburgh Hall, Norfolk.

A Dish of Scotch Collops

'Take a Legg of Veale and slice it very thin, then beat them to make them tender, then shred a little Orange Pill very small, then mix a little thyme with them, and so season. Then frye them. When they are fryed very well, beat some yolks of Eggs, and a little wine, and so put them into the frying pan, and toss all together, and so dish them and lay some shred Lemon upon the Top and garnish your dish with what you think fit.'

From Elizabeth Birkett's commonplace book, 1699

Collops was the old word for slices of meat and this dish is 'after the French fashion'. Wafer-thin slices of lamb, mutton or veal were rapidly stir-fried before being immersed in rich, piquant sauces of wine, spices and highly flavoured items such as garlic, onions and anchovies. The dish was often accompanied by forcemeat balls and was usually served at the first course of dinner.

The Balls for the Collops

'Take some lean veal and so mach pound them very well with a bit of Lemmond rind, a little onion and a few sweet herbs. Season it with pepper and salt, then put to it, two eggs and mix it up; roll it into little balls and fry them.'

From a bundle of 40 recipes written by various hands and thought to have belonged to Sarah Lowry Corry who married Galbraith Lowry of Castle Coole, Co. Fermanagh in 1733. Although the recipe is early 18th-century, it is very similar to 17th-century recipes for forcemeat balls.

Scotch Collops with Forcemeat Balls

2 lb (1 kg) frying steak
3 oz (75 g) butter
1 oz (25 g) flour
¾ pt (450 ml) beef stock
¼ pt (150 ml) dry white wine
1 teaspoon (5 ml) fresh thyme, chopped
thinly cut peel of 1 orange, preferably a Seville
a little shredded lemon peel to garnish

FOR THE FORCEMEAT BALLS

6 oz (175 g) fresh white breadcrumbs
2 oz (50 g) shredded suet
2 oz (50 g) lean veal, minced or bacon, finely chopped
1 tablespoon (15 ml) parsley, chopped
1 teaspoon (5 ml) fresh thyme, finely chopped
grated rind of ½ lemon
salt and freshly milled black pepper
1 large egg, beaten
1½ oz (40 g) butter or lard for frying

Although the original recipe uses veal, it is not easy to buy today, so I have used frying steak. Cut the steak into strips of about 5 × 2-ins (13 × 5-cms) and ¼-in (5-cm). Melt the butter in a large frying pan and fry the collops of meat for a few minutes on each side until evenly brown. Transfer to a large shallow saucepan or sauté-pan. Stir the flour into the frying-pan juices and cook for a few seconds, then add the stock gradually, stirring continuously, followed by the wine, the thyme and the orange peel. Bring just to the boil so that it thickens to the consistency of thin cream, then pour over the collops.

Prepare the forcemeat balls. Mix together the breadcrumbs, suet, veal or bacon, herbs, lemon rind, and seasoning, then stir the beaten egg into the mixture. Form into 12 small balls about 1-in (2.5-cm) in diameter. Melt the fat in a frying pan, and fry the forcemeat balls for about 6 minutes, or until brown. Add to the collops, season to taste, and cover. Simmer gently for about 10 minutes.

Arrange the collops and forcemeat balls on a warm serving dish and discard the orange peel. Pour over the sauce and serve immediately, garnished with a little shredded lemon peel. Serves 6.

To Make Potted Hare

'After it is Baked, beat it well in a mortar with some of the Liquor and about 7 ounces of Butter, season it with mace, nutmeg, pepper and Salt, according to the size of the Hare, put it close into pots, and Cover it an Inch thick with Butter, then set them in the Oven for about a Quarter of an Hour, the Oven must not be too Hot.'

Erddig ms 2551 (a), c.1765

Although this recipe dates from the middle of the 18th century, the method was the same in the 17th. Potting became a popular way of preserving meat, game and fish, and potted food was a fashionable dish at the tables of the well-to-do, served among the lighter fare of the second course.

To Fry Parsnips

'Let the parsnips be first tender boyled, and if they be thick cleave them, being peeled, then strew a little bit Cinamon on them, and put them to steep in little Sack, ffry them in a little butter. Make sauce, with butter, Sack and Cinamon beat together and they will eat well.'

From Elizabeth Birkett's commonplace book, 1699

Ordinary folk satisfied their sweet tooth by using honey and dried fruits, which were much cheaper than sugar, and fresh fruits and vegetables rich in natural sugars. Parsnips, like carrots, skirrets and sweet potatoes, were popular.

Glazed Parsnips

1 lb (450 g) parsnips, scrubbed and trimmed
salt
2 oz (50 g) butter
1 teaspoon (5 ml) honey
juice of 1 large orange
2 tablespoons (30 ml) lemon juice
1 tablespoon (15 ml) sweet sherry or Madeira
generous pinch of ground cinnamon
generous pinch of ground mace or nutmeg
freshly milled black pepper

Boil the parsnips in salted water for 12–15 minutes, or until just tender. Drain thoroughly and leave to cool. Peel them and slice off the thin root ends, leaving them in one or two pieces. Slice the thicker ends in half lengthwise. Put the butter, honey, orange and lemon juice and sherry into a wide, heavy pan. Stir over a low heat. When the butter has melted, stir in the cinnamon and mace or nutmeg. Place the pieces of parsnip in the pan, turning them to coat them with the buttery juices. Season with salt and pepper, then cook over a low heat, partially covered, until the parsnips are golden brown and have absorbed all the juices. Serve hot. Serves 4–6.

Potted Hare

8 oz (225 g) cooked hare, minced
6 oz (175 g) clarified unsalted butter
pinch each of ground mace, nutmeg, and black pepper
little salt if necessary

Reduce the cooked meat to a paste with 4 oz (125 g) of the clarified butter in an electric blender or food processor. Season to taste with the spices, pepper and salt. Press firmly into a small earthenware or china pot and chill. Heat the remaining clarified butter and pour over the meat to seal. (A thinner layer of butter – for appearance rather than preservation – will be enough if you plan to use the potted hare in a day or two.) Covered with foil it will keep for at least a month in the fridge. Serve with thin wholemeal toast. Serves 6 as a starter.

Beef, salt beef, veal, tongue and venison may all be potted in the same way and can be served instead of pâté as a starter. Potted meats also make delicious sandwich fillings.

An early 17th-century still-life by a French or Flemish painter, at Kingston Lacy, Dorset, showing a kitchenmaid with vegetables and game.

A Compound Sallat

'Take a good quantity of blanched almonds cut coarsely. Then take as many raisins of the sun clean-wasshed and the stones pikt out; as many figs shred like the almonds; as many capers; twice as many olives, and as many currants wasshed clean as all of the rest. Add a good handful of small, tender leaves of red sage and spinach. Mix these all together with a good store of sugar. Lay them in the bottom on a dish, then put unto them vinegar and oyl. Then take oranges and lemons and cut them into thynne slices. Then with those slices cover the sallat over. Cover the oranges and lemons with thinne leaves of red cole-flower, then over these red leaves lay another course of old olives and the slices of well-pickled cucumbers together with the inward hearts of cabbage lettice cut in slices.'

From *The Accomplisht Cook*, Robert May, 1660

Seventeenth-century salads were dressed in patterns as complicated as the contemporary knot gardens. Gervase Markham advised laying out salads for a special occasion to look like bunches of flowers – 'some full blown, some half blown and some in the bud'. Compound salads were first-course dishes and were also popular for suppers.

A Spinage Tart

'Take a good quantity of spinage and boyle it, and when tis boyled, put it into a Cullender, that the water may run out from it, then shred it very small, and season it with good flow of sugar, and a pretty quantity of melted butter, then put in yolks of Eggs, and beat them altogether. Then make a sheet of paste very thin, and put it upon a Dish; so put your Tart Stuff upon it, then another sheet to cover it ...'

From Elizabeth Birkett's commonplace book, 1699

To Make Pufe Past

'Take a quart of the finest flouer and the whites of three egges and the yolks of fore and a litel colde water and so make it in to past. Then drive it with a roling pine. A broad this put on smale peces of buter, then folde it over. Drive it thine againe. Doue this tenne times always folding the paste and puting buter betwene.'

Erddig MS 1203, *c*.1685

Sweet spinach tarts were popular in 17th-century England. Some included dried fruit, usually currants, almond macaroons, spices and rose-water, and many were iced with rose-water and sugar. They were served at the second course of dinner.

Spiced Spinach Tart

8 oz (225 g) shortcrust or puff pastry
2 lb (900 g) fresh or frozen spinach
4 oz (125 g) butter
4 eggs
2 tablespoons (30 ml) rose-water
1 teaspoon (5 ml) sugar
good pinch of ground ginger
good pinch of grated nutmeg
salt and freshly milled black pepper

Line a 9-in (22-cm) loose-bottomed flan tin with the pastry and bake blind for 10–15 minutes.

Meanwhile, cook the spinach gently in just the water that clings to the leaves after washing. Drain very thoroughly by pressing out the juice in a colander and dry over a low heat. Melt the butter in another saucepan and add the spinach, stirring until it is mixed well. Beat the eggs with the rose-water, sugar, spices and seasoning. Remove the spinach from the heat and add the egg mixture, stirring well. Taste and adjust the seasoning as necessary. Tip the mixture into the pastry case and bake for 10 minutes in a fairly hot oven (200°C, 400°F, gas mark 6), then turn the heat down to 190°C, 375°F, gas mark 5, and bake for a further 20–30 minutes, or until the filling is well-risen, set and lightly browned on top. Serve warm. Serves 6–8.

Compound Salad

Place a variety of salad leaves including spinach or sorrel, shredded red cabbage and herbs on a large flat dish as a base to the salad. Arrange on top slivers of blanched almonds, chopped figs, large stoned raisins, capers, currants and sliced green olives, then finish with a layer of thinly sliced oranges, lemons and pickled cucumbers. Decorate with thickly sliced lettuce hearts. Serve with a vinaigrette dressing.

An illustration from Robert May's *The Accomplisht Cook*, showing cut-laid tarts. These were served at the banquet with their upper crust removed after cooking and replaced by separately baked, patterned tart-tops of rich puff paste.

Raspbery Creame

'Take a quart of Creame put it to boyle. Beat the whites of 3 Eggs well, and when it hath boyled well, put in your Eggs with a Leafe of Mace and a slice of Lemon pill. Boyle it till it thicken, season it with sugar, then strain it, and beat it well in your dish, then haveing your Rasberryes well stewed, mix them with your Creame, stir it with some of the Juice of them, you must also put in some Amber, and serve it up.'

From Elizabeth Birkett's commonplace book, 1699

Creams and butters formed an important part of the banquet, being either spooned from their dishes, scooped up with wafers, or eaten with brown bread. Creams were also combined with fruit such as gooseberries, pippins, quinces and raspberries to give pleasantly sharp dishes.

To Make a White-Pot

'Take three quarts of Cream, and put into it the yolks of twelve Eggs; the whites of four, being first very well beaten between three quarters of a pound of Sugar, two Nutmegs grated, a little Salt; half a pound of Raisins first plump'd. These being sliced together, cut some thin slices of a stale Manchet; dry them in a dish against the fire, and lay them on the top of the Cream, and some Marrow again upon the bread, and so bake it.'

From *The Closet of the Eminently Learned Sir Kenelm Digbie, Kt. Opened*, 1669

Cookery books revealing recipes from the closets of the aristocracy were extremely popular in the 17th century. Sir Kenelm Digby was a prominent figure at the Stuart Court. He married the celebrated beauty and courtesan Venetia Stanley, previously kept by Richard Sackville, the 3rd Earl of Dorset as his concubine and mother to a number of his children. The Earl of Dorset invited the married couple to dinner once a year, when he 'would behold her with much passion yet only kiss her hand'.

Sir Kenelm Digby's recipes are attributed to specific friends and acquaintances ranging from professional cooks to high-ranking members of the aristocracy, but there is little sign of the 'haute cuisine' of France. The dishes are for the most part quite ordinary, using ingredients that would be abundant on any country estate. White pot was one of the popular creamy dishes of the period and ancestor of our modern bread and butter pudding. It was usually served during the second course at dinner or as a supper dish.

Raspberry Cream

¾ pt (450 ml) double cream
few blades of mace
long strip of lemon peel
1 oz (25 g) caster sugar
1 egg white
¾ pt (450 ml) lightly sweetened raspberry purée

Boil the mace, lemon peel and sugar with most of the cream for a few minutes until well-flavoured. Beat the egg white with the remaining cream, then mix into the hot sauce. Boil up twice, stirring frequently before straining through muslin into a bowl. Leave to cool. When cold, stir in the raspberry purée. Taste and add extra sugar if necessary, although the dish should be on the sharp side. Pour into a serving dish and chill. Serve with puffs (see p.36). Serves 6–8.

Bread and Butter Pudding

3 oz (75 g) raisins
1 tablespoon (15 ml) sherry
4 thin slices bread, well buttered and crusts removed
grated rind of 1 lemon
freshly grated nutmeg
2 oz (50 g) caster sugar
¾ pt (450 ml) single cream
3 eggs, beaten

Soak the raisins overnight in the sherry.

Next day, prepare the pudding several hours before you want to cook it, to allow the bread to soak up some of the cream and eggs. Cut the buttered bread into triangles. Butter a 2-pint (1-litre) ovenproof dish and scatter a few of the soaked raisins over the bottom. Fill the dish with layers of bread sprinkled with grated lemon rind, grated nutmeg and the remaining raisins, finishing with bread and grated nutmeg. Heat the cream slowly until just reaching boiling point. Leave to cool a little, then pour over the beaten eggs, stirring continuously with a balloon whisk. Stir in the sugar, then ladle this over the waiting bread carefully, so that the pieces are not disarranged. Leave to stand for as long as possible, but at least 2 hours.

Place the dish in a roasting tin with warm water to come half-way up the side of the dish, then bake in the centre of a moderate oven (180°C, 350°F, gas mark 4) for 30–40 minutes, or until the custard is just set and the bread crisp and golden. Serve warm with cream. Serves 6.

To make a Rare Scillybub

'Take a quart of Creame, a pint & half of white wine or Sack, the Juice of 2 Lemons with some of the piell and a branch of Rosemary, Sweeten it very sweet, then put a Little of this Liquer and a Little of the Creame in to a bason. Beat it till it froths, put the froth into the Scillybub and do until the Creame and wine be done, then Cover it Close and let it in a Coole celler, if it stand there 12 houres it will be the better; if you please you may putt in a Little Ambergrese in to the wine.'

From the Arundell family papers. From the 13th to the middle of the 18th century, the Arundells were one of the great families of Cornwall, with one branch of the family established at Trerice by the reign of Edward III. The family archives have recently been acquired jointly by the County Councils of Cornwall and Wiltshire.

Syllabub was a confection of white wine, cider or fruit juice, well-seasoned with sugar and flavoured with lemon, spices or rosemary, to which milk or cream was added with considerable force. Some recipes recommended that the milkmaid milked the cow directly on to the liquor to produce a frothy head with a clear liquid below. The latter was drunk from the miniature spout of special two-handled syllabub glasses, while the creamy foam was eaten as a spoonmeat. The following recipe is for the more solid type of syllabub.

Everlasting Syllabub

thinly pared rind and juice of 1 lemon
2 oz (50 g) caster sugar
¼ pt (150 ml) medium dry sherry or white wine
sprig of fresh rosemary
½ pt (300 ml) double cream

The day before the syllabub is to be made, put the thinly-pared rind and juice of the lemon in a bowl with the sugar, sherry or white wine and the sprig of rosemary. Cover and leave overnight to let the flavours develop.

Next day, strain the liquid into a large deep bowl and stir in the cream, gradually beating it with a wire whisk until it holds its shape. Be careful not to over-beat or the cream will curdle. Spoon into small glasses – preferably stemmed or custard cups – and serve immediately or keep in a cool place overnight. Decorate each glass with a tiny sprig of rosemary, or a little twist of lemon peel and serve with jumbles (see p.26). Serves 4–6.

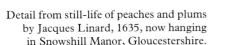
Detail from still-life of peaches and plums by Jacques Linard, 1635, now hanging in Snowshill Manor, Gloucestershire.

To Make Puffs

'Take a pound of double refined sugar, beat and sift it fine, then take 2 graynes of Amber greese finely beaten, and mix it with the sugar, then take the White of an Egg, and beat it till it be all a froth.
So put in your sugar by degrees, and beat it as you would do Biskett, then take a pretty quantity of Coriander or Carrowayes, put them in And roll it up in little Balls about the bigness of a Nutmegg and lay it upon Wafers, and set them round like Loaves and bake them.'

From Elizabeth Birkett's commonplace book, 1699

Various forms of light sponge biscuit were served at the 17th-century banquet as a crisp, delicate and bland foil to all the rich fruit- and sugar-based dishes. These puffs, or early meringues, were also known as White Bisket Bread, often flavoured with ground almonds, coriander, aniseed, caraway seed, lemon peel or chocolate.

Spiced Meringues

2 egg whites
4 oz (125 g) caster sugar
1 teaspoon (5 ml) ground coriander

Whisk the egg whites until they form stiff peaks and are smooth, then whisk in 2 teaspoons of the sugar. Fold in the remaining sugar and the coriander with a metal spoon. Brush a baking sheet lightly with sunflower oil and line with a sheet of Bakewell paper. Drop small spoonfuls of the meringue mixture on the baking sheet. Dredge with a little extra caster sugar, then place in a very cool oven (125–135°C, 250–275°F, gas mark ½–1) for about 1 hour, until crisp and delicately beige in colour.

To make a Great Cake

'Take 3 pound and a halfe of flower, 2 pound and a halfe of Currans, halfe a pound of Raisons of your sun stoned, halfe a pound of sugar, halfe a pint of Rose Watter, a pint of Creame, a pound of fresh butter, a Gill of Ale barme, yolks of 10 Eggs and 3 whites. Let the Creame boyle and put in the Butter to melt in it, beat 9 Eggs and mingle with the barme, Rose Watter and sugar. Pour in the Cream and butter, and stirr it well together, then take halfe an ounce of Mace, well beaten and throw upon it, then take some of the flower and strew over it, and let it stand till it hath wrought over, then work it together, put in your fruit, and when it is wrought until it will come from your hands in the Bowle, lay it upon a sheet of White Paper buttered, and a browne one under it and let it stand in the Oven an houre, then take some whites of Eggs, melted butter and Rose Watter, beaten together, and wash your Cake over with a bunch of Sage, and throw over it sugar, and let stand in the Oven a little longer.'

From Elizabeth Birkett's commonplace book, 1699

Cakes were still enormous in the 17th century, round or oval in shape and containing prodigious amounts of dried fruit. Rose-water was frequently used by cooks instead of water, which was often of dubious quality.

Yeast Fruit Cake

1 oz (25 g) dried yeast
7½ fl oz (225 ml) warm water
2 eggs
3 oz (75 g) caster sugar
pinch of salt
10 oz (275 g) butter, melted
¼ pt (150 ml) double cream, warmed
1 tablespoon (15 ml) brandy
1 tablespoon (15 ml) orange juice
1 lb (450 g) plain flour
½ teaspoon (2.5 ml) ground mace
½ teaspoon (2.5 ml) ground cinnamon
1 teaspoon (5 ml) freshly grated nutmeg
8 oz (225 g) currants
8 oz (225 g) raisins

FOR THE GLAZE

1 tablespoon (15 ml) caster sugar
1 tablespoon (15 ml) rose-water
1 tablespoon (15 ml) melted butter

Dissolve the dried yeast in the warm water and leave in a warm place to froth (10–15 minutes). Beat the eggs with the sugar and salt, then beat in the melted butter followed by the warm cream, the frothy yeast mixture, the brandy and the orange juice. Sieve the flour and spices into a large mixing bowl, then add the fruit. Stir in the egg and yeast mixture and mix well. Cover with a piece of oiled cling film and leave to prove in a warm place for about 30 minutes.

Meanwhile, grease and line a deep 8-in (20-cm) diameter cake tin. Wrap a double thickness of brown paper around the tin and tie securely with string (this prevents the sides of the cake burning). Preheat oven to 190°C, 375°F, gas mark 5. Turn the cake mixture into the prepared tin and level the top. Bake in the centre of the oven for 1–1¼ hours, covering the top of the cake with greaseproof paper after the first 15 minutes to prevent it burning.

To make the glaze, dissolve the sugar in the rose-water over a low heat, then stir in the butter. Brush over the cake immediately after removing it from the oven, then leave to cool in the tin.

Wrap in greaseproof paper and leave to mature for at least 24 hours before cutting. Makes an 8-in (20-cm) round cake.

To Make Past of Apricocks

'Take your Apricocks and pare them, and take the stones out of them put them into a Pot and cover them close, sett them into a Kettle of Watter, and let them stand infusing in it 2 or 3 hours, then take them and strayne them through a Sieve, then put to a pound of your Pulpe of Apricocks halfe a pound of the Pulpe of boyled Pippins, then clarify a pound of Sugar, and boyle it to a candy height, and put your Pulpe of Pippins and Apricocks into it. Keep it stirring over the fire till it comes cleane from the bottom of the Pan, then lay it upon plaites, dry it and keep it for use.

From Elizabeth Birkett's commonplace book, 1699

Stiff pastes or marmalades of fruit pulp and sugar, made firm enough to be cut into squares or modelled into decorative shapes, were still served at the Stuart banquet. Alongside the earlier quince marmalades, recipes using apricots, oranges, lemons, peaches and pippins were becoming popular.

My Lord of Carlile's Sack-Possett

'Take a Pottle of Cream, and boil in it a little whole Cinnamon, and three or four flakes of Mace. To this proportion of Cream put in eighteen yolks of Eggs, and eight of the whites; a pint of Sack; beat your Eggs very well, and then mingle them with your Sack, Put in three quarters of a pound of Sugar into the Wine and Eggs with a Nutmeg grated, and a little beaten Cinnamon; set the basin on fire with the wine and Eggs, and let it be hot. Then put in the Cream boyling from the fire, pour it on high, but stir it not; cover it with a dish, and when it is settled, strew on the top a little fine Sugar mingled with three grains of Ambergreece, and one grain of Musk, and serve it up.'

From *The Closet of the Eminently Learned Sir Kenelm Digbie Kt. Opened*, 1669

Sack posset provided the ideal 'warm-up' before travelling home after an evening out, or retiring to bed. It was spooned from beautifully decorated silver posset pots, or sipped from large earthenware vessels kept warm by the fire.

Sack Posset

9 egg yolks
4 egg whites
½ pt (300 ml) dry sherry
large pinch of ground cinnamon
large pinch of ground mace
½ teaspoon (2.5 ml) freshly grated nutmeg
2 pints (1.2 litres) single cream
6 oz (175 g) caster sugar

This delicious warming drink is especially good at Christmas. In a basin, beat together the egg yolks, egg whites, sherry and spices. Pour into a large saucepan and heat gently, stirring all the time until warm, but not thick. Heat the cream and most of the sugar in another saucepan and as they come to the boil, pour from a good height into the warm egg mixture. Allow to stand for a few minutes in a warm place, then sprinkle the reserved sugar over the surface, and serve in warm wine glasses or pottery goblets. Serves 10–12.

An earthenware posset cup, Lambeth *c.*1700, with an English delft charger, now in Lady Betty Germain's Closet at Knole, Kent.

Apricot Paste

½ pt (300 ml) apricot purée made from about
  1 lb (450 g) canned or cooked fresh fruit,
  or from 8 oz (225 g) dried fruit, soaked
  if necessary and cooked
8 oz (225 g) granulated sugar
2–3 teaspoons (10–15 ml) lemon juice
granulated or caster sugar to coat

Put the purée, sugar and lemon juice into a heavy-based saucepan and dissolve the sugar over a gentle heat, then bring the mixture to the boil and cook, stirring gently, for about 40 minutes, or until a little will set firmly on a cold surface. Wet an 8 × 6-in (20 × 15-cm) tin and pour in the mixture. Leave to set in a cool place. When the jelly is set, cut it into pieces and roll in granulated or caster sugar. Store in an airtight jar or tin until needed. Makes about 1 lb (450 g).

Georgian Food

For the fortunate few, the Georgian period was an age of gastronomic elegance – tables decorated with pyramids of edible pleasure; of sophistication – an Empire that encompassed exotic foods epitomised by the shipping of live turtles from the West Indies for turtle soup; and indulgence – like the friend of the diarist John Byng who regularly devoured twelve mutton chops for dinner.

The National Trust has several examples of Georgian kitchens, but perhaps the most elegant is at Kedleston Hall in Derbyshire, designed by Robert Adam in the 1760s. It is situated in a pavilion attached to the central body of the house – the temple of the arts – partly to keep a distance between cultural contemplation and cooking smells, partly to reduce the hazard of fire. The latter was only too likely – the kitchen at Saltram in Devon was moved into a separate block in 1788 following a fire.

Saltram's roasting range of c.1800 has a hob grate, mechanical jacks and water tank to supply hot water on tap. The next logical step was to enclose the range, and Thomas Robinson took out a patent for this in 1780. An example of one of his ranges, still in working condition, is in the Park Farm House at Shugborough in Staffordshire. Stew hearths were another important component of the Georgian kitchen; they were very effective for the controlled cooking of sauces with roux (see the fricassée recipe, p.42) and for soups with thickenings (p.40)).

In earlier centuries, professional cooks were men: women began to make their appearance in the kitchen only in the later 17th century. But in Georgian times they were remedying this with a vengeance, inspired by a series of women cookery writers: Eliza Smith, *The Compleat Housewife*, 1727; Hannah Glasse, *The Art of Cookery made Plain and Easy*; Elizabeth Raffald, *The Experienced English Housekeeper*, 1769.

When Mary Smith, formerly housekeeper to Sir Walter Calverley Blackett at Wallington in Northumberland, published her cookery book, *The Complete Housekeeper*, in 1772, she suggested dinner menus for different months of the year. For a second course in July she includes cucumbers, peaches and melons. Exotic fruit and vegetables had been imported since the Middle Ages, but could not be home grown until the late 17th century when glasshouses and orangeries were added to houses. The orangery at Felbrigg in Norfolk was built right at the beginning of the 18th century, while the one at neighbouring Blickling was designed in the 1780s by Samuel Wyatt.

Pineapples represented the pinnacle of fruit in Georgian fashion. First introduced into England during the reign of Charles II, they could be raised in pineries, special hot-houses, but were expensive and difficult to grow, and therefore a great treat. When pineapple failed to materialise at a dinner at Saltram in October 1811, the Rev. Thomas Talbot wrote to his wife in considerable tones of disapproval.

For the ice-creams (p.46) and iced puddings that were to be such a feature of Georgian – and Victorian – desserts, the hot-house linked up with two other features of the country-house estate: the ice-house and the dairy. The ice-house usually consisted of a brick-lined dome over a well, with the sides sloping inwards to a sump. In winter ice would be taken from ponds, loaded into the well with layers of straw to insulate and keep through the summer. Good 18th-century ice-houses can be seen at Felbrigg and Ham. The dairy at Shugborough, home of the Anson family, is based on the Tower of the Winds in Athens. The maid would produce cream and butter in the basement, while Lady Anson and her friends played at dairymaids in the chamber above, making flummeries and junkets.

Breakfast in leisured Georgian households was taken between 9 and 11, often in a new feature, the Breakfast or Morning Room. The Rev. Talbot, in another of his letters to his wife, describes the Morning Room at Saltram, 'an Urn and cistern of black tea at one end – ditto of green at the other, and coffee on the side.' Generally breakfast was a light meal of bread and butter, muffins, spiced bread or small cakes.

Luncheon makes its appearance in the 18th century: an informal snack, an accidental happening between meals, consisting at first of cakes or biscuits with beverages or wine. Later, it became more substantial, with cold meats, pies and salads.

The dining-rooms at Kedleston and Saltram were both designed by Robert Adam, with a buffet or sideboard at one end to carry the dishes, wine-coolers and at Kedleston, a magnificent perfume burner. Dinner was still the main meal of the day, of two courses plus a dessert, now taken at the table. The cloth would be removed, and the bare mahogany table covered with dishes of fresh and preserved fruit, jellies and syllabubs (pp.47 and 35), often using pyramids of glass salvers piled up in the centre. Once dessert was over, the ladies retired for coffee, 'tea and scandal', leaving the men to settle the nation's destiny, toast their mistresses and drink themselves under the table.

The Morning Room at Saltram.

To Make Asparagus Soup

'Take a Hundred of Asparagus, put the Greatest part of them with two Lettuces into three Quarts of Water – Boil them till they are tender enough to pulp thro' a Cullender; they should be Boil'd two or three Hours after they are put thro' the Cullender, add the remainder of the Asparagus, put some Cream and flour to make it a Sufficient thickness, and add pepper and Salt, to your taste – The Asparagus you put in last are to Swim in the Soup.'

From an Erddig recipe book, *c*.1765

Philip Yorke I of Erddig was a vegetarian so would have enjoyed this soup.

To Stew Soals

'Cut them across with a knife, fry them in Clarified butter, then put them in a Stewpan then pour over them Clarrett two or three Anchovies let it stew till tis enough. Squeese in the juice of a Lemon, thicken it up with Butter.'

From an 18th-century recipe book at Montacute

As it was still difficult to get fresh sea-fish in the 18th century, frying it and adding strong flavourings was a well known way of masking any unpleasant tainting.

To Stew Cucumbers

'Cut them in Slices and drain them well, shake them in a Frying pan, with some Brown'd Butter, then put in some pepper, salt and some Onions sliced, some Gravy, Stew them 'till they are enough, Squeeze in some Lemon, Thicken them up as you do other Dishes'.

From an Erddig recipe book *c*.1765, as recommended by Mrs White

Eighteenth-century recipe books abound with recipes for 'stew'd', 'farc'd', baked and 'ragout' of cucumber. Stewed cucumber was served with roast meat.

Asparagus Soup

about 1 lb (450g) fresh asparagus
½ lettuce, washed
1 small onion, finely chopped
1½ pt (900ml) vegetable or chicken stock
1 oz (25g) butter
¾ oz (18g) plain flour
2 egg yolks
2½ fl oz (about 75 ml) double cream
salt and black pepper

Cut off the tips from the asparagus and reserve for garnishing. Trim the asparagus and cut into 1-in (2.5-cm) pieces. Shred the lettuce finely, then put it with the asparagus and onion in a pan. Pour over the stock, cover the pan and simmer gently until the asparagus is tender. Put through a blender or food processor to make a purée. Steam or simmer the asparagus tips very gently until tender, drain and reserve. Rinse out the pan, then make a roux with the butter and flour, and stir in the purée. Season well, then gently bring to the boil and simmer for a further 2–3 minutes. Mix the egg yolks and cream together and stir into the soup. Reheat carefully without boiling, then taste and adjust seasoning as necessary. Add reserved asparagus tips and serve hot. Serves 4–6.

Sole in Red Wine with Anchovy

4 fillets of sole, skinned
salt and black pepper
clarified butter for frying
4 dessertspoons (40ml) melted butter
2½ fl oz (75ml) claret
4 anchovy fillets
squeeze of lemon juice
lemon slices and deep-fried
    parsley sprigs, to garnish

Season the sole fillets with salt and pepper. Melt a little clarified butter in a large frying pan and fry the fish lightly on both sides, adding more butter as necessary. Remove from the heat and pour off any remaining fat. Add the melted butter and the claret and arrange the anchovy fillets on top of the fish. Cover the pan and set over a very low heat for about 5 minutes, or until the fish is cooked through. Squeeze over a little lemon juice and serve immediately, garnished with lemon slices and parsley sprigs fried in deep fat (a very common 18th-century garnish for fish). Serves 4.

Ragoût of Cucumber

2 medium cucumbers
2 oz (50g) clarified butter
2 medium onions, sliced
6 tablespoons (90ml) chicken stock
2 tablespoons (30ml) dry white wine
salt and pepper
beurre manié to thicken

Slice the cucumbers thickly without peeling them. Melt half the butter in a pan and brown the cucumber lightly. Meanwhile, melt the remaining butter in another pan and brown the onions lightly. When the onions have softened, add them to the cucumber. Add the stock and wine and season well. Cover with a lid and simmer until tender. Remove the lid and thicken with beurre manié until the vegetables are nicely bound together by a little sauce. Check the seasoning again and serve. Serves 6.

To Make Mushroom Patties

'Cut off the Stalks of large Mushrooms close, Skin & Gill them, Season them with pepper & Salt, then dip them in good Batter, fry them in Pork, Beef or Mutton fat – when they are of a Nice light Brown they are Enough –
NB they are Nice to eat with Chicken or Veal.'

From an Erddig recipe book *c*.1765, as recommended by Mrs White

Mushroom Fritters

1 lb (450 g) small flat or button mushrooms
salt and freshly milled black pepper

FOR THE BATTER

4 oz (125 g) plain flour
½ teaspoon (2.5 ml) salt
¼ pt (150 ml) lukewarm water
2 tablespoons (30 ml) olive oil
2 egg whites
oil for frying
sea salt or grated cheese, to finish

About 1 hour before you wish to serve the fritters, make the batter. Sieve the flour and salt into a basin and make a well in the centre. Gradually beat in the lukewarm water until a smooth batter is formed, then beat in the oil. Leave to rest for 1 hour. Wipe the mushrooms with kitchen paper and sprinkle with salt and pepper.

When you are ready to cook the fritters, heat the oil for deep-frying to 180°C, 350°F. Whisk the egg whites until stiff but not dry, then fold gently into the prepared batter. Dip the mushrooms briefly in the batter using a skewer and shake off any excess. Fry a few at a time for about 5 minutes, turning over once, until golden brown. Drain on kitchen paper and serve very hot, sprinkled with sea salt or grated cheese. Serves 4 as a main course or 8 as a starter.

Silver soup tureen from Ickworth, Suffolk. It was made for George Hervey, 2nd Earl of Bristol, by Frederick Kandler in 1754.

Chicken or Rabbit Fricassée

A Fricassee of Chickens or Rabbits

'Cut the Chickens or Rabbits out and lay them into cold water to soak, or if you are in hast warm and wash them well, so set them over in water in a stew-pan on the fire till they are boiled enough, then take them out of the liquor and strain it through a sieve that it may not be discoloured so wash the stew-pan and put in the meat with the liquor that you strained with three or four blades of mace. Set on the fire then having ready a cup of cream the juice of half a lemon, two yolks of eggs, beat up together very well with a little salt, take a little of your hot liquor about a spoonfull and mix with it and by degrees put it all in and either shake or stir it with a spoon till it is thorough hot so serve it up.'

From an 18th-century manuscript found at Canons Ashby

Dishes of French origin, like the fricassée, were still very popular, but were now made with a thickened sauce to envelop the meat.

4–6 chicken or rabbit joints
chicken stock or water, to cover
2 medium onions, sliced
1 bouquet garni
salt and black pepper
2 oz (50 g) mushrooms
½ oz (15 g) butter

FOR THE SAUCE

1½ oz (40 g) butter
2 tablespoons (30 ml) flour
1–2 egg yolks
¼ pt (150 ml) single cream
squeeze of lemon juice
slices of lemon, to garnish

Put the chicken or rabbit joints in a shallow pan, cover with stock or water and add the sliced onions and bouquet garni. Season well. Cover and simmer for about 40 minutes, or until very tender. Drain off the cooking liquor into a measuring jug, cover pan again and keep hot. The stock should measure 1 pt (600 ml); if it is more, turn into a saucepan and reduce. To prepare the sauce, melt the butter in a separate pan, stir in the flour, cook for a few seconds, without letting the butter brown, then pour on the stock and stir in well. Cook over a gentle heat stirring all the time until thick. Boil briskly for 3–4 minutes, and then draw aside.

At the same time, sauté the mushrooms in butter in another pan. To finish the sauce, mix the yolks with the cream in a bowl, add a little of the hot sauce, then pour the mixture slowly back into the rest of the sauce. Check the seasoning again and add the lemon juice and mushrooms. Pour the sauce over the joints, shaking the pan gently to mix all together. Cover and keep hot for 15 minutes before serving, so that the flavour of the sauce can penetrate the meat. Garnish with lemon slices. Serves 4–6.

Potato Pudding

To Make a Potatoe-Pudding

'Take 12 oz of Potatoes pound them very fine in a Mortar [with] 12 Yolks of Eggs, 4 Whites, 12 oz sugar, 12 oz of butter, some Mace and Cynnamon dry'd and powdered – a Spoonful or two of Brandy, as much Citron as you please. A Quarter of an Hour will bake it, put it in puff paste – round the brim.'

From an 18th-century recipe book at Montacute

Potatoes, like carrots, spinach, and artichokes were often made into sweet puddings in the 18th century to serve alongside the meat and fish in the first course at dinner.

6 oz (175 g) shortcrust pastry
2 oz (50 g) butter
2 oz (50 g) caster sugar
3 oz (75 g) potatoes, cooked and mashed
good pinch of ground mace
good pinch of ground cinnamon
grated rind of 1 lemon
1 large egg and 1 large egg
  yolk, beaten together
1 tablespoon (15 ml) brandy

Line a 6-in (15-cm) flan ring with the pastry and bake blind in a hot oven (220°C, 425°F, gas mark 7) for 10–15 minutes. Leave to cool.

Cream the butter and sugar until white and fluffy. Beat in the mashed potatoes, spices and lemon rind, followed by the egg mixture and the brandy. Taste and add more spice if you wish. Spoon into the pastry case and bake in a moderate oven (180°C, 350°F, gas mark 4) for about 45 minutes or until risen and golden. Serves 4.

Oyster Loaves

Oyster Loaves

'Take small french rolls, or round loaves, make a hole in the top, take out the crumb, then fry them in butter, and set them before the fire to dry, Stew your Oysters in their own liquor, add the crumbs out of your rolls, and a good piece of butter, stew then 5 or 6 minutes, then put in a spoonful of Cream, fill the loaves and lay on the top.'

From an Erddig recipe book *c*.1765, as recommended by Mrs Hazel

These made 'a pretty Side-dish for a first Course' according to Hannah Glasse. The dish was taken to America and became popular in New Orleans in the 19th century. Oysters were also eaten fresh, fried, 'ragoo'd' or made into sauces and stuffings.

4 miniature cottage loaves or brioches
4 oz (125 g) butter, melted
12 fresh oysters
salt and black pepper
good pinch of grated nutmeg
¼ pt (150 ml) double cream
a little lemon juice

Cut the tops off the rolls or brioches and scoop out most of the crumb. Brush the undersides of the lids and the hollows of the rolls inside and out with butter. Place on a baking sheet in a hot oven (220°C, 425°F, gas mark 7) for about 10 minutes, or until lightly golden and crisp. Meanwhile scrub and open the oysters and drain off the liquor, reserving it. Sauté the oysters in the remaining butter, in a frying pan, for about 1½ minutes, or until they turn opaque. Remove oysters from the pan with a draining spoon, cut them into 2 or 3 pieces, depending on size, and set aside. Add the reserved oyster liquor to the pan with the seasonings and cream. Boil down steadily to a very thick sauce, stirring constantly. Check the seasoning, sharpening with a little lemon juice if you wish, reheat the oysters in the sauce gently and spoon into the warm rolls. Replace the lids and serve immediately for a special first course, or supper dish. Mussels, cockles or mushrooms could be used instead. Serves 4.

The Oyster Lunch by Jean-François de Troy, 1734. England was acknowledged by all – including the French – as the home of the finest oysters in the 18th century. At this feast, prodigious numbers are being consumed, accompanied by champagne. The sealed corks of the bottles are held down by tape and string. Fine export bowls are used to cool and rinse out the glasses. Note the stiletto-bladed knives used in France, and so complained about by English travellers.

Creamy Macaroni Cheese

Maccaroni and Cheese

'Boil half a pound of maccaroni in water 'till quite tender, drain it on a Sieve, then put it into a Stew-pan with a piece of butter, a little grated cheese, and a little gravy, set it over the fire to stew for ten minutes, add a little pepper, salt and nutmeg to your taste; put it in a china dish, with half a pound of Parmazan cheese grated on the top, – set it in an oven for fifteen minutes, then take it out and brown it with a salamander, and serve it up in a second course.'

From *The Complete House-Keeper and Professed Cook etc*, Mary Smith, 1772

First known in England in the 14th century, this dish was apparently not made again until the 18th century, when it returned from Italy. A hot salamander – an iron, disc-shaped utensil with a long handle – was held over the top of the dish to brown the cheese, or failing this, a heated fire-shovel was recommended.

4 oz (125 g) wholewheat macaroni
2 pt (1.25 litres) water
1 teaspoon (5 ml) salt
2 oz (50 g) butter
1½ oz (40 g) plain flour
1 teaspoon (5 ml) dried English mustard
¾ pt (450 ml) milk
5 oz (150 g) Cheddar cheese, grated
salt and freshly milled black pepper
freshly grated nutmeg
1 oz (25 g) Parmesan cheese, grated
1 tablespoon (15 ml) fresh wholemeal breadcrumbs

Cook the macaroni in boiling salted water for 10–15 minutes or until just tender. Meanwhile, melt the butter in another pan, stir in the flour and mustard, and cook for a few seconds without browning. Add the milk gradually to make a white sauce and cook for about 5 minutes, then stir in half the Cheddar cheese. Let it melt gently into the sauce, then season with salt, pepper and nutmeg. Drain the cooked macaroni in a colander and combine it with the sauce. Turn into a lightly buttered 2-pint (1.2-litre) baking dish. Sprinkle the remainder of the Cheddar cheese, mixed with the Parmesan and the breadcrumbs, on top. Place under a preheated hot grill until golden brown and bubbling. Serves 2.

Decanter and wine glasses decorated with Jacobite emblems, c.1750, from Chastleton House, Oxfordshire. A tax assessed according to weight had been placed on glass in 1745, encouraging the development of decoration. Henceforward beauty of design and cutting, engraving and gilding dictated value.

Eighteenth-century Trifle

The 17th-century trifle of thickened cream seasoned with sugar, ginger and rose-water had now become more substantial, with Naples biscuits or macaroons, custard and a syllabub topping. It was served for the second course at dinner, or for supper.

FOR THE BASE

18 boudoir biscuits or sponge fingers
3–4 tablespoons (45–60 ml) medium dry sherry or white wine

FOR THE CUSTARD

½ pt (300 ml) double cream
3 large egg yolks
1 level teaspoon (5 ml) cornflour
1 oz (25 g) caster sugar

FOR THE TOPPING

finely grated rind and juice of 1 lemon
4 tablespoons (60 ml) medium dry sherry or white wine
1 teaspoon (5 ml) orange-flower or rose-water
2 oz (50 g) caster sugar
½ pt (300 ml) double cream
redcurrant or blackcurrant jelly to decorate
finely shredded orange, lemon or citron peel to decorate

Several hours before you want to serve the trifle, prepare the liquor for the syllabub topping. Put the lemon rind and juice, sherry or wine, orange-flower or rose-water and caster sugar into a bowl. Cover with cling film and leave for a few hours to let the oils from the rind impregnate the liquor.

Meanwhile make the custard. Heat the cream in a small, preferably non-stick, saucepan. Beat the egg yolks with the cornflour and sugar in a small basin until smooth, then pour on the hot cream, stirring all the time. Return the custard to the pan and stir it with a wooden spoon over a low heat until thick. Place the pan on a cold surface or in a bowl of cold water to remove any heat which might curdle the custard. Leave to cool while you prepare the base.

Break the biscuits in half and place in the bottom of a pretty shallow glass or china dish. Sprinkle over the sherry or wine, then pour over the waiting custard. Cool completely.

To make the topping, strain the prepared liquor into a clean bowl and stir in the cream, gradually beating it with a rotary or balloon whisk until it stands in soft peaks. (Be careful not to overbeat or the syllabub will separate.) Decorate with small blobs of jelly and candied peel. Serve chilled.

NB This trifle is exceedingly rich and small portions should be served. Serves 6–8.

Orange-flavoured Caraway Cake

Eighteenth-century cakes and biscuits were mostly eaten as accompaniments to wine between or after meals.

6 oz (175 g) butter or soft margarine
6 oz (175 g) caster sugar
3 large eggs
grated rind of ½ orange
1 tablespoon (15 ml) caraway seeds
6 oz (175 g) self-raising flour
1 tablespoon (15 ml) orange juice

Preheat oven to 180°C, 350°F, gas mark 4. Cream the fat and caster sugar until white and fluffy. Beat the eggs and add gradually to the creamed mixture, beating well after each addition. Stir in the orange rind and caraway seeds, then sieve the flour into the creamed mixture. Fold in gently with the orange juice, then spoon into a greased and lined 2-lb (900-g) loaf tin. Bake in the oven for 45–55 minutes, or until firm to the touch. Cool on a wire rack.

Orange Ice Cream

'Squeeze the juice of eight sweet oranges in a bowl, add to it half a pint of water, and as much sugar as will sweeten it; strain it through a sieve, put it into an ice well, and freeze it 'till it is stiff; put it into a lead pine-apple mould, lap it well up in paper, put it into a pail of ice, and salt under and over it, and let it stand for three hours. When you want it, dip your pine-apple in cold water, turn it out on a plate, green the leaves of the pineapple with spinach juice, and garnish it with green leaves. You may put this cream into melon and pear moulds. If a melon, you must green it with spinach juice; – if a pear mould, you must streak it with red.'

From *The Complete House-keeper and Professed Cook, calculated for the greater Use and assistance of Ladies, House-keepers, Cooks, etc.* written by Mary Smith and published in 1772. She had been housekeeper to Sir Walter Blackett at Wallington in Northumberland – it was common for servants to write and publish cookery books.

No fashionable dessert course was served without ices in Georgian times. They could be made at home if you were lucky enough to have an ice-house; if not, confectioners in the largest towns sold a huge variety, for which they had their own stores of ice. Pineapple moulds were particularly popular, because the fruit was a symbol of luxury in the 18th century.

To Make Chocolate Creem

'Take a pint of good Creem, an heaped spoonfull of Chocolate scraped, put it in when the Creem boyls, stir them well together, beat the yolk of 2 eggs and stir it into the Creem, sweeten it to your tast, let the Eggs have a boyl or two to thicken it, put it into a Chocolate pot and Mill it, so hold the Pot high and pour it into a dish.'

From an 18th-century manuscript from Canons Ashby, as recommended by Mrs Martyn

This rich cream made from the fashionable chocolate would have been 'milled', or frothed, with a chocolate mill or molinquet, 'a wooden stick with an head at the end full of notches', and served at the second course.

Plums from *Pomona Franconia* by Mayer, 1776.

Chocolate Cream

6 oz (175 g) plain chocolate
2–3 tablespoons (30–45 ml) water
½ oz (15 g) butter
2–3 drops of vanilla essence
3 large eggs, separated
¼ pt (150 ml) double cream

Break the chocolate into small pieces, put in a saucepan with the water and stir continually over very gentle heat until a thick cream. Take off the heat and stir in the butter and vanilla essence, followed by the egg yolks, one at a time, stirring well after each addition. Whisk the egg whites to a firm snow, then stir briskly into the chocolate. When thoroughly mixed, fill 6 small pots or glasses and leave overnight in the cool. Serve with small biscuits. Serves 6.

Orange Ice-cream

1¼ pt (750 ml) water
15 oz (425 g) granulated sugar
finely grated rind and juice of 1 large lemon
finely grated rind and juice of 8 large oranges
drop of red food colouring

Bring the water and sugar to the boil in a heavy saucepan, adding the grated lemon and orange rind as the syrup is heating up. Leave the syrup to boil for exactly 1 minute, then remove from the heat immediately and add the strained lemon and orange juice and food colouring. When the syrup is cold, strain, then set to freeze. After 1 hour, remove and beat thoroughly. Repeat until the mixture begins to harden into ice-cream, which will take 4–5 hours, unless using an ice-cream machine when it will only take 30–45 minutes.

The Duchess of Montagues Receipt to Make Hartshorn Jelly

'Put in one Gallon of watter half a pound of Hartshorn. Let them boyl slowly till the Liquor is a pretty strong Jelly, then strain it off and put in two Quarts of that, the peel of eight oranges and four lemons cut very thin, boyl it a quarter of an hour, then put in the whites of 12 eggs, well beat up in a froth all the Juice of the Oranges and Lemons, and a pound and a quarter of double refined Suger, boyle it a little and then strain it through a Flannell Bagg. You may put wine in it if you wish.'

From an 18th-century manuscript found at Canons Ashby

Jellies set with shavings of hartshorn and calves' feet, and served in glasses, were a popular part of the dessert course. They began to be flavoured with lemon and orange juice in the 18th century.

Lemon Jelly

1¾ oz (45 g) gelatine
1½ pt (900 ml) water
pared rind and juice of 3 large lemons
7 oz (200 g) lump sugar
2 egg whites, and the shells of the eggs, wiped and lightly crushed
2½ fl oz (75 ml) white wine

Soak the gelatine in ¼ pt (150 ml) of the water. Pour the remaining water into a scalded pan, add the lemon rind, juice and sugar. Warm over gentle heat until the sugar is dissolved. Whip the egg white to a froth, add to the pan with the shells, the gelatine and the white wine. Whisk until the liquid reaches boiling point. Allow to boil up three times, drawing the pan aside between each boiling to allow it to settle. Pour the liquid into a scalded jelly bag with a bowl underneath. Return the liquid several times to the jelly bag until it runs crystal clear. Pour into a mould or into glasses and leave to set. Makes 2 pt (1.2 litres) of jelly.

To Make Ramokins

'Take a Quarter of a pound of Cheshire Cheese, two Ounces of Butter beat together in a Mortar, then lay'd onto a Butter'd Toast. Crisp it with a Salamander.'

From a recipe book at Erddig c.1765

This was a very popular supper dish in the 18th century, particularly in Wales. For the English version, the toast was soaked in red wine.

Savoury Cheese Toast

2 oz (50 g) butter
8 oz (225 g) Cheshire or Cheddar cheese, grated
salt and pepper
2 egg yolks if required
4 slices bread, lightly toasted

Melt the butter in a heavy saucepan, stir in the cheese and season well. Stir over a gentle heat until the cheese melts. If the mixture shows signs of separating, bind together again with the egg yolks. Spread the toast with the mixture and brown under preheated grill for 3–4 minutes. Serve immediately. Serves 2 or 4.

The conservatory at Tatton Park, Cheshire, designed for the Egerton family by Lewis Wyatt and built 1820. This watercolour by Buckler was commissioned to celebrate its completion.

Victorian and Edwardian Food

Mrs Beeton, in her very influential *Book of Household Management*, 1861, likened the kitchen to a 'great laboratory' and this theme is echoed right through the Victorian era and beyond. The architect C. B. H. Quennell writing in 1911 called the kitchen offices of a large house a 'modern factory'. This is not a fanciful notion – households could be huge, and the cook needed to cope with four to five meals a day, plus separate dishes for the nursery and the servants' hall.

Lanhydrock in Cornwall is an excellent example of such a household. Rebuilt in 1883 by the Clifden family after a disastrous fire, its service quarters take up more space than that allotted for the family use. The kitchen, which has the look of an Oxbridge college hall, satisfies the recommendations laid down by Mrs Beeton: a large room with facilities that are convenient and easy to use; good lighting and ventilation; distance from the rest of the house to cut down on odours and noise; access from outside for the delivery of supplies, fuel and water.

The hearth remained the central feature of the Victorian kitchen, now fitted with a cast-iron range. The open type was effective for heating the room but expensive on fuel – Cragside in Northumberland has a good example. The closed range came later, but by 1900, 90 per cent of homes were fitted with them. There are two closed ranges side by side at Shugborough and Wallington in Northumberland; one would be set at low heat for simmering soups and stews, the other fired up to roast or bake. At Saltram there is a free-standing type known as a 'Leamington kitchiner'. The great chef Alexis Soyer introduced gas stoves to the Reform Club in London in 1841, but it took another thirty years for them to be adopted domestically. The first electric stoves came to the United Kingdom in 1894; by 1910 there were 10,000 in service.

The British Empire reached its zenith in the 19th century, and this is reflected in the diet of the Mother Country. Eliza Acton's *Modern Cookery Book*, 1845, and Mrs Beeton's *Household Management* were aimed at middle-class households who wanted to follow the latest fashionable trends. Foodstuffs from all over the world were imported by retail chains like the Home & Colonial Stores, co-founded in 1878 by Julius Drew. So successful was the enterprise that Drew retired at the age of 33 and commissioned an ambitious country home, Castle Drogo in Devon, from the architect Edwin Lutyens. Anglo-Indian dishes proved particularly popular on Victorian tables (recipes, p.50), though I have not included Mrs Beeton's curious imperial amalgam, curried kangaroo tails.

Victorians regarded eating well almost as a duty, and took advantage of every social occasion to do so: shooting lunches, cricket teas, picnics, supper balls. Breakfast became a substantial meal and could include grilled meats, roasted birds, kidneys and fish. Tea as a meal made its appearance, introduced by Anna, Duchess of Bedford, who got 'a sinking feeling' in the mid-afternoon. Moving out of the boudoir and into the drawing-room in the 1850s, tea became a grand five o'clock event with lots of cakes (pp.56 and 57) and biscuits on offer.

According to the anonymous aristocratic author of *Manners and Tone of Good Society*, 1879, formal dinner parties were 'first amongst all entertainments ... having more social significance and being more appreciated by society than any other form'.

The ideal Victorian and Edwardian dining-rooms were solid, masculine affairs, as opposed to the essentially feminine drawing-room. Good examples may be seen at Penrhyn Castle, Gwynedd and Charlecote Park, Warwickshire (1840s), Cragside (1870s), Wightwick Manor, West Midlands and Lanhydrock (1880s), and Castle Drogo (1912). In such sombre surroundings a revolution took place in dining. The service now known as *à la française* had basically remained the same since the Middle Ages: two courses with dishes placed on the table at the same time, followed by a dessert. In the 1860s fashionable society adopted the custom in Russia of laying the table with complete place settings while servants brought in the sequence of courses. *A la russe* required fewer servants to wait at table but was heavier on table-ware, giving the chance to display one's opulence. It also meant for the first time that the food could be served hot.

Once all these courses were consumed, ladies retired, leaving the men at table to drink claret, port and coffee, but it was no longer fashionable to linger. Formal dinners usually ended at 10.30pm, when carriages were called. Mrs Beeton, ever mindful of regulation, warned: 'It is well to remember that early rising is almost impossible if late going to bed be the order, or rather the disorder of the house.'

The late 19th-century kitchen at Cragside.

Rice à la Sœur Nightingale

'Fry the boiled rice with a little fresh butter, nutmeg, pepper and salt; and when quite hot, add the whites of three hard-boiled eggs shred fine, and the white parts of a dried haddock; pile all this up lightly in a hot dish; strew over the cone the yolks of the hard-boiled eggs previously rubbed through a wire sieve, and mixed with a little grated Parmesan cheese; garnish the rice round the base with fried croutons of bread, push in the oven for five minutes – just to slightly colour the surface of a golden hue, and serve immediately.'

From *The Cook's Guide*, Charles Elmé Francatelli, 1862

The practice of naming new dishes after well-known personalities was popular in Victorian times. The great chef Francatelli honoured Florence Nightingale when he named after her his new dish of Kedgeree (an English version of an Indian dish called *Khichiri*), for British-Indian cuisine was a chic novelty at London's dining-tables. It became a popular Victorian breakfast and supper dish.

Malecotony Soup

'To two Quarts of good Broth, add a little Ham, some Allspice, Mace, Cloves, Thyme, Marjoram, Basil and Onions. Boil all these together for one Hour adding two tablespoonfulls of Curry powder with a very little flour and butter. Pass it all thro' a Sieve and add to it a Chicken cut in small pieces with a *little* Garlic and Lemon (two cloves of Garlic and one good Lemon). Boil it half an Hour which will be sufficient to dress the chicken; Rice must be boiled very dry to eat with it – one pint of Patna Rice should be boiled in just one pint of Water. When it has just boiled up, it should be put at a distance from the fire (not to burn) and being covered close up, the steam will finish doing it.'

From a small book found on the shelves in Disraeli's study at Hughenden Manor, Buckinghamshire, alongside his wife Mary Anne's diaries/account books. The recipes, in either Mary Anne's or her housekeeper's hand, are mixed with household and gardening hints and remedies – even for distemper in dogs.

Malecotony or Mulligatawny Soup was a fashionable Victorian soup originating in southern India and deriving its name from the Tamil *milagutannir* meaning pepper-water.

Mulligatawny Soup

1 small fresh chicken
3 oz (75 g) butter
2 medium onions, chopped
1 tablespoon (15 ml) mild curry powder
1 garlic clove, crushed
1 tablespoon (15 ml) flour
3 pt (1.8 litres) cold water
8 oz (225 g) lean ham, chopped
4 whole cloves
2 large blades mace
sprig each of thyme, basil and marjoram
juice of 1 large lemon
salt and freshly milled black pepper
sour cream or yoghurt
boiled rice to serve

Cut the chicken into pieces and brown all over in the butter in a large flameproof casserole. Remove to a plate while you fry the onions. Stir in the curry powder and garlic and cook for a few minutes, then stir in the flour and continue to cook for another few seconds. Gradually stir in the water, then return the chicken to the casserole. Add the ham, cloves, mace, herbs, lemon juice and seasoning and bring to the boil. Simmer for 1–1½ hours or until the chicken is tender, then remove it and discard all the skin and bones. Return all the meat to the casserole, discarding the cloves, mace and herbs. Taste and adjust the seasoning as necessary, then reheat and pour into a tureen. Swirl in a little sour cream or yoghurt. Serve with a separate bowl of boiled rice. Serves 6–8.

Florence Nightingale's Kedgeree

1 lb (450 g) smoked haddock, cooked
3 eggs, hard-boiled
1 tablespoon (15 ml) Parmesan cheese, grated
3 oz (75 g) butter
6 oz (175 g) long grain rice, cooked
salt and freshly milled black pepper
freshly grated nutmeg
small triangles of fried bread to garnish
1 tablespoon (15 ml) fresh parsley, chopped

Remove the skin and bones from the fish and flake coarsely. Chop the whites of the hard-boiled eggs and add to the fish. Press the yolks through a sieve and mix with the cheese. Melt the butter in a saucepan and toss the rice in it over gentle heat until well coated and heated through. Mix in the fish and egg whites and gently continue to toss until the whole mixture is hot. Season with salt, pepper and nutmeg, then pile onto an ovenproof plate. Scatter the egg yolk and cheese mixture on top and place under a gentle grill for a few minutes until the cheese begins to colour. Arrange the triangles of fried bread around the rice and sprinkle with parsley. Serve immediately. Serves 4–6.

A 19th-century grocer's bill heading.

Crimped Salmon with Dutch sauce or Salmon Hollandaise

'To dress salmon or trout in perfection in this style, it is quite necessary that the fish be dressed a short time after being caught. If it be practicable to procure what is termed a *live salmon*, take out the gills, draw out the guts, &, wash the fish and crimp it on either side, by making deep incisions with a very sharp knife, and then throw it into a large tub containing clean, cold, spring-water, fresh from the pump; the water to be changed every half-hour, and the salmon to remain in it for about two hours. In crimping any sort of fish, the colder the water is the better; the coldness of the water petrifying the fish to a certain degree, gives it the firmness so much desired. Put the crimped salmon on to boil in hot water, with a good handful of salt; allow it to boil gently on the side of the stove, remembering that all crimped fish require considerably less time to boil than plain fish. As soon as the fish is done, it should be immediately drained from the water, dished up on a folded napkin; garnished round with picked parsley, and served with Dutch sauce.'

Dutch Sauce

'Four yolks of raw eggs, two ounces of fresh butter, half a gill of cream, a very small quantity of nutmeg, pepper, and salt, and a teaspoonful of elder vinegar:- having put the foregoing ingredients into a small stewpan, place it within another stewpan of rather larger size, containing half a pint of hot water, and then, after placing the sauce in its bath over the fire, proceed to work it swiftly, either with a wire whisk or small wooden spoon, until it begins to thicken and present a rich, smooth, creamy appearance. Great care must be taken to prevent this sauce from curdling and becoming decomposed, which may be prevented by not stirring it over too fierce a fire. If, however, this accident should occur, by adding either two more yolks, or a spoonful of white sauce, it will be remedied.'

From *The Cook's Guide*, Charles Elmé Francatelli, 1862

Crimped fish was a very popular English speciality in Victorian and Edwardian times. The method of preparation was applied particularly to salmon, cod, haddock and skate, but the fish had to be straight out of the water as it would have been at Penrhyn Castle. Lord Penrhyn had nets across the Menai Straits and the salmon was so abundant that his servants complained they had too much salmon to eat. Even if salmon could not be caught locally, by the middle of the 19th century it was being shipped regularly from Scotland packed in ice. Victorians and Edwardians would have used a whole salmon for this dish and used up the leftovers in hashes, rissoles and cutlets.

Poached Salmon Hollandaise

2½–3 lb (1.2–1.4 kg) piece of salmon
a little melted butter

FOR THE SAUCE

4 tablespoons (60 ml) white wine vinegar
6 black peppercorns
1 blade mace
1 slice of onion
1 small bayleaf
3 egg yolks
5 oz (150 g) unsalted butter, slightly soft
salt and freshly milled pepper
1 tablespoon (15 ml) single cream
squeeze of lemon juice (optional)
cucumber and fennel or dill to garnish

Brush a piece of foil large enough to wrap up the salmon with melted butter. Season the foil generously, then lay the fish on top and wrap into a parcel. Fill a fish kettle or large pan half full of water and bring it to the boil. Lower the parcel of salmon into the water, bring back to the boil, then simmer for about 15 minutes until cooked; bearing in mind that the thickness of the fish will vary the cooking time. Keep the fish warm in the foil while making the sauce.

To make the sauce, put the vinegar into a small saucepan with the spices, onion and bayleaf. Boil until reduced to a scant tablespoon, then set aside. Cream the eggs yolks in a bowl with a good knob of butter and a pinch of salt. Strain on the vinegar mixture, set the bowl over a pan of boiling water, turn off the heat and add the remaining butter in small pieces, stirring vigorously all the time. When all the butter has been added and the sauce is thick, taste and adjust the seasoning as necessary. Add the cream, and lemon juice if desired. The finished sauce should have the consistency of thick cream.

Serve the salmon decorated with cucumber slices and sprigs of fennel or dill and the sauce separately. Serves 6.

Homard à la Crème

'Cut up the live lobster and put these pieces into a sautépan containing $\frac{1}{6}$ pint oil and 1 oz butter, both very hot. Fry them over an open fire until the pieces of lobster are stiffened and coloured, then clear them of all grease; swill the sautépan with 1 tablespoon burnt brandy, and add, immediately, 4 oz. fresh, peeled truffles cut into slices.

Moisten, almost sufficiently to cover, with very fresh, thin cream; season with salt and cayenne, and cook the lobster. Then take the meat from the carapaces, and put it into a timbale [a metal dish]; reduce the cream to $\frac{1}{3}$ pint, and mix therewith 3 tablespoonfuls melted, white meat-glaze and a few drops of lemon-juice. Strain this sauce through muslin, and pour it over the pieces of lobster.'

From *A Guide to Modern Cookery* by the famous French chef Escoffier, first published in 1907. His recipes were frequently inspired by those of the 14th-century French chef, Taillevent; so we have travelled the full circle.

This lobster dish epitomises the extravagance of the Edwardian era.

Lobster in Cream

$1\frac{1}{2}$–2 lb (750 g–1 kg) lobster cooked in court
   bouillon and cut into neat pieces
1 oz (25 g) butter
1 sherry glass of brandy
2 egg yolks
$\frac{1}{2}$ pt (300 ml) double cream
salt and freshly milled pepper
$\frac{1}{2}$ teaspoon (2.5 ml) paprika

Heat a frying or sauté pan and grease well with butter. Put in the lobster pieces, then season and heat gently for 2–3 minutes. Pour over the brandy and set alight. Draw aside. Beat the egg yolks, then add the cream and season well with salt, pepper and paprika. Stir quickly into the lobster and shake above the heat, stirring gently all the time until the sauce is thick and creamy. (Be very careful that it doesn't boil or it will curdle.) Serve lobster at once with boiled rice. Serves 3–4.

Haricot Mutton

'2 lb Neck or Loin of Mutton
1 pt water, 1 carrot, $\frac{1}{2}$ turnip
1 onion, small tablespoonful of Flour,
   salt and pepper

Cut into chops & cut most of the fat from them, fry them in a little dripping, put them into a pan after they are browned nicely. Pour on the water slightly warm, cover closely, bring to a boil & let it cook gently. Clean & cut the vegatables into small pieces, fry them in the same dripping that the chops have been done in, add them to the chops. Let it cook gently $1\frac{1}{2}$ to 2 hours. Mix the flour with a little cold water & stir into the haricot, season it, alow it to boil up then the dish is ready.'

From a hand-written recipe book belonging to Mrs Straw

The Straw family owned a grocer's shop in Worksop in Nottinghamshire. At first they lived 'above the shop' in Market Square, but as they prospered, moved into a semi-detached Edwardian villa, 7 Blyth Grove, in 1923. Mrs Straw started her recipe book in 1880 and must have used it all her married life until 1939, as the pages seem well-thumbed. She was a keen and good cook, who attended cookery lectures at one time. Her son William, who took over the housekeeping after her death, lists a number of recipes under this heading.

Mutton was a very popular meat in Victorian times, although it is now almost unobtainable. It has a stronger taste than lamb, but lamb may be used instead.

William Straw, grocer and seed merchant, stands outside his shop in the Market Square in Worksop, Nottinghamshire. The Straw family lived above the shop until 1923 when they moved to No.7 Blyth Grove.

Haricot of Lamb

2 lb (1.2 kg) middle neck of lamb or mutton
   divided into cutlets
2 onions, peeled and quartered
1 small piece swede or turnip
2 carrots
1 oz (25 g) dripping or butter
1 tablespoon (15 ml) flour
$\frac{3}{4}$ pt (450 ml) stock or water
salt and freshly milled black pepper
1 bouquet garni

Trim most of the fat from the cutlets, removing any superfluous bone and cut the onion, swede and carrots into short thick strips. Heat the dripping in a flameproof casserole until smoking, then brown the cutlets on both sides. Remove with a slotted spoon and reserve, then fry the vegetables until they are just coloured. Stir in the flour and cook for a minute or two, then stir in the stock or water. Bring gently to boiling point, replace the meat in the casserole and make sure that the liquid comes just level with the meat. Season well, add the bouquet garni, then cover with a lid. Simmer gently for about 1 hour, or until the meat is tender, turning the cutlets from time to time. Serve with creamed potatoes. Serves 4.

Kromeskies

'Kromeski is a Polish word, which means no more than the French croquette, and which in its first syllable might find a fair equivalent in the English crumb. If it were lawful to invent a word, it might be translated crumbikins. The kromeski or Polish croquette is made in the usual way with an addition. It is any croquette formed into a little roll and wrapped round with a thin slice of the udder of veal, or failing that with thin bacon. The veal udder (which is always best) or the bacon is boiled beforehand, is then sliced and wrapt round the croquette, which is finally dipped into batter and consigned to the frying-pan, from which it should come out crisp. This is the most seductive of all forms of croquette.'

From Kettner's *Book of the Table*, E. S. Dallas (first published anonymously)

Batter for Kromeskies of Chicken

'2 oz Flour, ½ tablespoon of salad oil & one egg, a little & half a quarter of a pint of water add the yoke of the egg and oil to the flour and stir the water in smoothly let it stand half an hour whisk the white of the egg to a stiff froth and stir smoothly into the batter before you want to use it. fry the parsley in the frying basket in fat a few minutes to garnish the dish.'

From a hand-written recipe book belonging to Mrs Straw

Between dinner parties, most Victorians ate leftovers for which there were numerous recipes. 'Kromeskies' was one of the more delicious, 'made of chicken, game, sweetbreads, fat, livers, oysters, shrimps – and generally the lighter kinds of meat' according to Kettner's *Book of the Table*. Auguste Kettner, once Napoleon III's chef, owned a very successful restaurant in Soho and had long been friendly with the distinguished journalist E. S. Dallas, the 'anonymous' author of the *Book of the Table*.

Polish Croquettes

1 medium-sized onion
4 oz (125 g) mushrooms
1 oz (25 g) butter
4 oz (125 g) fresh white or brown breadcrumbs
2 egg yolks
2 tablespoons (30 ml) double cream
salt and freshly milled black pepper
freshly grated nutmeg
8 oz (225 g) cooked chicken, turkey or ham, finely chopped
16 rashers of thinly cut smoked streaky bacon

FOR THE BATTER

6 oz (175 g) plain flour
pinch of salt
½ pt (300 ml) lukewarm water
1 dessertspoon (10 ml) salad oil
2 egg whites
oil for frying
sprigs of fresh parsley, fried, to garnish

Chop the onion and mushrooms finely and cook gently in butter for a few minutes until soft, but not browned. Mix with the breadcrumbs, egg yolks and cream, then season to taste with salt, pepper and nutmeg. Stir in the finely chopped meat.

De-rind the bacon, if necessary, and stretch the rashers with the back of a knife. Cut each one in half, spread it thickly with the stuffing mixture and roll it up. Arrange on a plate and put in the fridge to become firm.

To make the batter, sieve the flour and salt together in a bowl. Make a well in the centre and pour in the warm water. Gradually beat the flour into the liquid until the mixture forms a smooth batter. Beat in the oil, then leave to rest for about 1 hour.

When ready to make the croquettes, whisk the egg whites until stiff, but not dry. Fold them lightly into the batter. Heat the oil for deep-frying to 180°C, 350°F. Dip the prepared croquettes individually into the batter, shaking off excess mixture and deep-fry them, a few at a time, turning them over once, until they are golden brown (about 5 minutes). Drain on kitchen paper and serve very hot garnished with sprigs of fried parsley. Serves 4 as a snack for lunch or supper, or 8 as a starter.

Potatoes 'à la Maître d'Hôtel'

'Boil the potatoes in water, then peel them. Put some butter in a saucepan, with chopped parsley, pepper and salt. Toss in the potatoes; add a squeeze of lemon-juice, and serve at once. 1 pound of potatoes will require three-quarters of an ounce of butter.'

From *Wholesome Cookery*, Mary Beale, 6th edition, 1895

Mary was the sister-in-law of James Beale of Standen in Sussex. In the preface the author says that the menus and recipes have been carried out in a small household, with one cook and without the assistance of a kitchen maid. She advises the mistress of the house to provide her 'plain cook' with a *Mrs Beeton* or an *Eliza Acton*, the author of *Modern Cookery*, published in 1845, and the first English cookery writer to sum up the ingredients and method at the end of a recipe in a few lines. Mrs Beeton copied the idea, placing them at the head of each recipe as we do today.

Potatoes were served at all meals of a fashionable household and it was *de rigueur* to serve them in a different way each time. This recipe shows the influence of hotels and restaurants on domestic cooking.

Stewed Rump of Beef

'INGREDIENTS. – ½ rump of beef, sufficient stock to cover it, 4 tablespoonfuls of vinegar, 2 tablespoonfuls of ketchup, 1 large bunch of savoury herbs, 2 onions, 12 cloves, pepper and salt to taste, thickening of butter and flour, 1 glass of port wine.

Mode. – Cut out the bone, sprinkle the meat with a little cayenne (this must be sparingly used), and bind and tie it firmly up with tape; put it into a stewpan with sufficient stock to cover it, and add vinegar, ketchup, herbs, onions, cloves, and seasoning in the above proportions, and simmer very gently for 4 or 5 hours, or until the meat is perfectly tender, which may be ascertained by piercing it with a thin skewer. When done, remove the tape, lay it into a deep dish, which keep hot; strain and skim the gravy, thicken it with butter and flour, add a glass of port wine and any flavouring to make the gravy rich and palatable, let it boil up, pour over the meat and serve. This dish may be very much enriched by garnishing with forcemeat balls . . .

Time. – ½ rump stewed gently from 4 to 5 hours.

Average cost. – 1s. per lb.

Sufficient for 8 to 10 persons.

Seasonable at any time.'

From *The Book of Household Management*, Mrs Isabella Beeton, 1861

A century of selective breeding and better animal nutrition had established British beef as the best in the world. Roast beef and 'beefsteak' were still the most popular dishes, especially for celebratory meals and gentlemen's lunches.

The dining-room at Erddig, Clwyd. The table is laid for dessert, as recommended by Mrs Beeton.

Sauté of Beef in Port

about 2¼ lb (1 kg) rump steak cut into 6 even-sized pieces
2 oz (50 g) butter
½ pt (300 ml) port
1 onion, finely sliced
2 garlic cloves, finely chopped
1 oz (25 g) flour
¾ pint (450 ml) beef stock
salt and freshly milled black pepper
1 bayleaf
2 sprigs of fresh thyme
4 cloves
1 lb (450 g) flat mushrooms
beurre manié, to thicken (optional)
fresh parsley, finely chopped, to garnish

Melt 1 oz (25 g) of the butter in a shallow, lidded pan and brown the meat, two pieces at a time, on both sides. Remove from the pan and put on one side. Pour the port into the pan, bring to the boil and boil until reduced by half. Pour over the meat. Melt the remaining butter and cook the onion and garlic until soft. Stir in the flour and cook slowly until straw-coloured. Blend in the stock and stir until boiling. Add the meat and port to the pan together with the herbs and cloves. Season to taste, then cover with a lid and simmer gently for 1 hour. Then, add the mushrooms to the pan and continue cooking for another hour, or until the meat is very tender. Remove the herbs and cloves and discard, then thicken if you wish, with *beurre manié*. Lastly, taste and adjust the seasoning if necessary. Serve sprinkled with chopped parsley. Serves 6.

Claret Jelly

'1 small bottle claret
1 cup of red currant jelly
¼ lb or less sugar
1 lemon, juice and rind, 1 oz isinglass
or a little more in Summer.

Simmer until the isinglass is dissolved.
Strain through muslin into a mould.
Stand until it is thoroughly cold and turn
out carefully into a glass or silver dish.'

From a recipe book dated 1888 which once
belonged to Parke near Bovey Tracey in Devon.

A sparkling wine-, liqueur- or fruit-
flavoured jelly set with isinglass (made
from the bladders of fish) or the newly
introduced gelatine was a popular sweet
entremet at the end of a Victorian dinner.
Sometimes a variety of fruits was set in
layers of jelly to make 'Macedoines'.
As iced puddings became more and more
fashionable, jellies were frozen for a
short time before being turned out and
sent to the table.

Cabinet Pudding

'Spread the inside of a mould with
butter; ornament the bottom and sides
with pieces of preserved fruits. Fill the
mould with alternate slices of sponge
cake, ratafias, and maccaroons, and some
more pieces of dried fruits, or small
lumps of guava jelly or apricot
marmalade. Made a custard with 7 eggs,
1 pint of milk, 6 ounces of sugar, and a
little vanilla or grated lemon-peel; add
1 wine-glassful of brandy. Let it get cold,
and pour it by degrees into the mould so
as to penetrate every corner; then cover
the mould and steam it an hour. Serve
cold with custard over it, into which mix
another wine glassful of brandy.'

From *Wholesome Cookery*, Mary Beale, 1895

Also known as Chancellor's Pudding,
this decorative dessert cream used up
stale sponge cake. It was on the
dinner menu with Charlotte Russe
on 19 December 1914 at Erddig, for
'a very gay Party notwithstanding poor
Philip's gout'.

Cabinet Pudding with Jam Sauce

a little unsalted butter
2 oz (50 g) glacé cherries, halved
1 oz (25 g) crystallised angelica
4 sponge cakes or 12 sponge fingers
1 oz (25 g) ratafias
4 eggs
1 tablespoon (15 ml) caster sugar
1 teaspoon (5 ml) cornflour
¾ pt (450 ml) single cream or milk
grated rind of ½ lemon
1 tablespoon (15 ml) brandy
2 oz (50 g) currants
2 oz (50 g) sultanas

JAM SAUCE

3 tablespoons (45 ml) apricot, strawberry or
    raspberry jam
6 tablespoons (90 ml) cold water
1 teaspoon (5 ml) lemon juice

Grease a straight-sided charlotte mould or
soufflé dish with unsalted butter and line the
bottom with buttered greaseproof paper or
foil. Decorate with the halved glacé cherries
and the angelica cut into diamond shapes.
Cut the sponge cakes into small squares and
arrange over the candied fruit in the mould,
with the ratafias crumbled into pieces on top.

Cream the eggs, sugar and cornflour together in a basin. Bring the cream and lemon
rind almost to the boil very slowly, then strain
over the egg mixture, stirring vigorously. Add
the brandy and dried fruit, then pour carefully over the cake in the mould. Leave to soak
for about 15 minutes; then cover tightly with
foil and tie down with string. Steam gently for
about 1 hour or until the custard is set and
firm. Allow to stand for a few minutes before
turning out very carefully on to a warm
serving dish. Remove the greaseproof paper
or foil from what is now the top of the
pudding.

To make jam sauce, melt the jam in a
saucepan with the water and lemon juice.
Push through a sieve to make it smooth.

Serve the pudding hot with a little jam
sauce poured around the base of the pudding
and extra sauce served separately. Serves 6.

Claret Jelly

1 pt (600 ml) claret
rind and juice of 1 lemon
1 oz (25 g) powdered gelatine
3–4 oz (75–125 g) granulated sugar
black grapes to decorate

Place 4 tablespoons (60 ml) of the claret and
the lemon juice in a small basin and stir in the
gelatine. If you wish to serve your wine jelly in
a bowl, 1 oz (25 g) gelatine will be sufficient,
but if you wish to turn it out of a fancy mould,
add an extra ½ oz (15 g) to make certain, but do
check quantities on the packet, because different makes can vary in strength. Leave for
5 minutes until swollen and soft, then stir this
into half the remaining claret in a saucepan.
Add the sugar and lemon rind, then bring
slowly almost, but not quite, to the boil,
stirring all the time. Strain into a bowl and
gently stir in the remaining claret. Pour into
a wetted mould, or into a pretty bowl and
leave to set in a cool place. Serve slightly
chilled, decorated with small bunches of black
grapes which have been frosted with egg
white and caster sugar and offer whipped
cream and ratafias with the jelly. Serves 6.

Iced Soufflé

'Mix in a saucepan 6 yolks of eggs, with 4 ounces of clarified sugar. Whisk this over the fire until it *nearly* boils; take it off the fire at once. Continue whisking till the mixture is nearly cold. Add to it 1 quart of whisked double cream and a glass of rum or curaçoa; continue whisking until all is thoroughly mixed. Have your soufflé lining standing on ice, so as to get it thoroughly cold; *this is important*. Fix a band of paper about 2 inches above the dish; pour in the mixture, almost as high as the paper; cover the mould completely and embed it in ice and salt. 2 hours' freezing is about the time it will take. Then take off the paper, strew biscuit powder lightly on the top, and serve. Soufflés can be flavoured with the juice of fruit, or coffee, or chocolate, or vanilla etc.'

From *Wholesome Cookery*, Mary Beale, 1895

With new freezing and chilling techniques it became possible for the rising middle class to serve ices and iced puddings as a grand finale to dinner.

Iced Raspberry Soufflé

6 oz (175 g) granulated sugar
2 fl oz (60 ml) water
3 egg whites
8 oz (225 g) fresh or frozen raspberries
few drops of lemon juice
½ pt (300 ml) whipping or double cream
few whole raspberries and fresh mint leaves to decorate

Cut a strip of greaseproof or Bakewell paper 3-in × 23-in (7.5-cm × 57.5-cm). Smear a little butter on the two ends, then wrap carefully round the top of a 7-in (18-cm) soufflé dish so that half the paper is below the rim and half is above. Press the edges together so that the butter sticks them, then tie the paper securely with string. Boil the sugar with the water until the syrup reaches 115°C (240°F) on a sugar thermometer. Meanwhile, whisk the egg whites until stiff. When the syrup has reached the required temperature, remove from the heat and immediately pour it in a thin thread on to the egg whites. Continue whisking until cold. Cook the raspberries over a gentle heat for a few seconds until the juices run, then liquidise and rub through a fine sieve to remove the pips. Add the lemon juice. Whip the cream until soft peaks form, then gently fold into the meringue together with the fruit pulp. Fill the prepared soufflé dish to the top of the paper and set to freeze. This will take about 5 hours.

When ready to serve, untie the string and remove the paper. Decorate with the reserved raspberries and mint leaves. Serves 6.

Recipe on Cooking Luncheon Cake

'1 lb flour
½ lb butter
1 lb currants
½ lb brown sugar
½ pint new milk or less of buttermilk
2 eggs
small teaspoon soda

Rub butter into flour and sugar. Mix soda thoroughly with the milk which must be cold, beat the eggs separately and mix in and bake immediately. Not to be done quickly it takes a long time.'

From some handwritten recipes found in the library at Springhill, Co. Londonderry

An informal lunch in Victorian times often finished with a plain fruit cake made with the newly invented baking-powder or baking-soda, instead of yeast.

Victorian Luncheon Cake

8 oz (225 g) plain flour
2 teaspoons (10 ml) baking powder
1 teaspoon (5 ml) mixed spice (optional)
4 oz (125 g) butter or margarine
4 oz (125 g) soft brown sugar
8 oz (225 g) currants
1 egg beaten
about ¼ pt (150 ml) milk

Preheat oven to 180°C, 350°F, gas mark 4. Sieve the flour with the baking powder and spice, if using, into a bowl. Rub in the fat with the fingertips until the mixture resembles breadcrumbs. Add the sugar and fruit, then stir in the beaten egg and enough milk to give a dropping consistency. Spoon into a greased 7-in (18-cm) cake tin and bake in the centre of the oven for about 1 hour, or until a skewer inserted into the cake comes out clean. Allow the cake to cool a little before turning out on to a wire rack. Makes a 7-in (18-cm) round cake.

After-dinner Savouries

'Angels on Horseback

Prepare very thin slices of bacon, roll them round one large or two small oysters, secure them with string and fry, then serve very hot on little rounds of fried bread.

Anchovy Olives

Prepare anchovy butter and fill Spanish olives with it. Set each olive on end on a little round of fried bread. The olives must be carefully stoned and hollow.

Sardine Savoury

On little square pieces of fried bread lay a little finely chopped salad. Moisten at the last moment with mayonnaise sauce. On this lay little thin slices of sardines.'

From a hand-written book of recipes entitled 'Extracts Memoranda' of about 1890 belonging to July Lucy Hoare of Stourhead House in Wiltshire.

It was fashionable in Victorian and Edwardian times to conclude the main part of dinner with a savoury, although Escoffier felt 'they had no place on a good menu'.

Felbrigge Sponge Cake

'¹⁄₂ lb sugar, ¹⁄₄ lb of flour, 7 eggs leaving out half the whites, the rind of half a lemon chopped fine, whisk it well and bake an hour and 10 minutes.'

From a small booklet of recipes, hints and remedies in various handwritings at Felbrigg Hall in Norfolk. Most of the recipes are anonymous dated about 1881.

This recipe is typical of the kind of light sponge or savoy cake popularly served for afternoon tea or among the sweet entremets or desserts for a grand dinner or banquet. The new wire egg-whisks introduced by the 1850s made beating eggs much easier and the cake would have been baked in a fancy tin mould.

Felbrigg Sponge Cake

Kitchen still-life at Arlington Court, Devon.

a little melted unsalted butter and a
    little caster sugar to prepare the tin
8 oz (225 g) caster sugar
finely grated rind ¹⁄₂ lemon
7 egg yolks
4 egg whites
4 oz (125 g) plain flour

Brush the inside of an 8-in (20-cm) diameter, deep sponge tin, or a 3–4¹⁄₂pt (1.75–2 litres) fluted mould with melted butter. Invert it and leave to drain and set, then sprinkle the inside with caster sugar, shaking out the excess.

Place the caster sugar and the grated lemon rind in a large bowl with the egg yolks. Beat with an electric hand-whisk or by hand, until the mixture is thick and almost white. In a separate bowl, whisk the egg whites with a clean whisk until stiff but not dry. Sieve a little of the flour into the egg yolk mixture and fold in with a large metal spoon. Then fold in about half the egg whites, followed by about half the remaining flour mixture. Repeat, using all the ingredients, then spoon as gently as possible into the prepared tin or mould. Bake in a moderate oven (180°C, 350°F, gas mark 4) for 1–1¹⁄₄ hours, or until the sponge feels firm and springy in the centre and has begun to shrink away slightly from the sides of the tin. Leave to cool in the tin for a few minutes, then turn out onto a wire rack to finish cooking. Sprinkle with caster sugar and eat as fresh as possible.

US CONVERSION TABLE

Information very kindly provided by the Good Housekeeping Institute

Dry Measures

1 US cup	=	50g	=	2oz of:	breadcrumbs; fresh cake crumbs
1 US cup	=	75g	=	3oz of:	rolled oats
1 US cup	=	90g	=	3½oz of:	desiccated coconut; ground almonds
1 US cup	=	100g	=	4oz of:	suet; grated hard cheese; walnut pieces; drinking chocolate; icing sugar; cocoa; flaked almonds; pasta; frozen peas
1 US cup	=	125g	=	5oz of:	white flour; self-raising flour; currants; museli; chopped dates; ground roasted nuts
1 US cup	=	150g	=	5½oz of:	wholemeal flour; raisins; cornflour
1 US cup	=	175g	=	6oz of:	apricots; mixed peel; sultanas
1 US cup	=	200g	=	7oz of:	caster sugar; soft brown sugar; demerara sugar; glacé cherries; lentils; long grain and brown rice; flaked and drained tuna fish
1 US cup	=	225g	=	½lb of:	cream cheese; cottage cheese
1 US cup	=	300g	=	11oz of:	mincemeat; marmalade
1 US cup	=	350g	=	12oz of:	syrup; treacle; jam

Liquid Measures

¼ US cup	=	60ml	=	2 fluid oz
1 US cup	=	240ml	=	8 fluid oz
2 US cups (1 US pint)	=	480ml	=	16 fluid oz

Butter, Lard and Margarine Measures

¼ stick	=	25g	=	2 level tablespoons	=	1oz
1 stick (½ US cup)	=	100g	=	8 level tablespoons	=	4oz

LIST OF PLATES

The author and publishers would like to acknowledge the institutions and individuals who have granted permission to reproduce their material in this book.

Please note that figures in **bold** refer to page numbers.

NTPL – National Trust Photographic Library
NT – National Trust regional libraries and archives

INDEX